PSYCHOLOGICAL
REPORTS
Second Edition

PSYCHOLOGICAL REPORTS

A GUIDE TO REPORT WRITING IN PROFESSIONAL PSYCHOLOGY

Second Edition

Raymond L. Ownby

CLINICAL PSYCHOLOGY PUBLISHING CO., INC.
BRANDON, VT

Copyright © 1987 by the Clinical Psychology Publishing Co., Inc.
Second Printing 1992
Second Edition.

Printed in the United States of America

ISBN 0-88422-019-2

Library of Congress Catalogue Card Number 91-70437

[CPPC] 4 Conant Square
        Brandon, Vermont 05733

ACKNOWLEDGMENTS

Acknowledgement is made to Lawrence Erlbaum Associates, Inc., for permission to reproduce figures 2, 3, and 4. These figures, as well as portions of several chapters, originally appeared in *Advances in School Psychology* (Vol. 5).

A number of persons assisted in the development of this book. In particular, I want to thank Fred Wallbrown for his continuing support of the project.

Acknowledgement also is made gratefully made to Fred Frese, Psychology Director, Western Reserve Psychiatric Hospital, Steve Rosenberg, Vice-President of PSI Associates, Cuyahoga Falls, OH, and Dan Guy, Clinical Director, Parkview Counseling Center, Youngstown, OH, for their assistance in collecting data used in studies discussed in this book.

Several persons read all or part of the manuscript; their comments are also acknowledged gratefully. These persons include: Fred Wallbrown, Associate Professor in the Counseling and School Psychology Programs, Kent State University, and Sally Felker, Assistant Director of Psychology, Western Reserve Psychiatric Hospital.

CONTENTS

Contents

PREFACE TO THE SECOND EDITION

In this second edition of *Psychological Reports*, I have attempted to build on the strengths of the first edition while improving the book in several areas. Although the conclusions advanced in this book remain in general empirically based, I have tried to made this edition more readable by rewriting much of it and by adding illustrative material.

The review of research literature has been updated; it was satisfying to discover that results of several recent research studies support theory-based recommendations made in the first edition. The book has been rewritten throughout with an eye to making many points clearer. A series of appendices has been added, which provide practice material for learning the model (Appendix A), a series of questions for self-diagnosing your reports and several questionnaires for eliciting feedback from consumers (Appendix B), and ways of describing test subtests or scales (Appendix C). The group of illustrative reports provided in the first edition has been retained, with one addition, in Appendix D.

Finally, I would like to acknowledge the helpful criticisms of the authors of reviews of the first edition: Gilbert Gredler (1987), David Hanson (1988), and Norman Sundberg (1989). Their thoughtful comments on the first edition of this book were very helpful in improving it in this edition. Although it was not always possible to alter the book to take into account every one of their criticisms, in many cases this edition has been changed to reflect their opinions.

I would also like to thank the staff of Clinical Psychology Publishing Company, especially Jerry Fuller, Ph.D., and Patricia Wood. Without their editorial and personal support neither edition of this book would have been possible.

The acceptance of the first edition has been gratifying. I hope that this second edition also will be useful to those of us who continue to work to improve our report writing.

1

INTRODUCTION

The Theory and Practice of Psychological Report Writing

The written report of an assessment is an important part of the psychologist's work, yet surprisingly little attention has been paid to determining what makes psychological reports useful and effective. This book's purpose is to give psychologists guidance in improving the way they communicate results of individual client assessments. The problem is approached by defining relevant questions about report writing and answering them on the basis of previous research. When research results are ambiguous or inadequate, expert opinion expressed in books or articles on psychological assessment is surveyed in order to determine whether a consensus on the point exists. Too often, as you will see, it has been necessary to rely on expert opinion because research on many important issues simply doesn't exist.

The dearth of research is perhaps due to the widespread devaluation by psychologists of assessment activities since the late 1950s; preference has been given in recent years to therapeutic activities. It may also be due to the general neglect of productive written language as a research topic (Britton & Black, 1985, p. 2) and to a lack of awareness on the part of psychologists of the importance and potential usefulness of preparing more effective reports. There have been relatively few empirical investigations of reporting in recent years, although recently there has been renewed interest (e.g., Pryzwansky & Hanania, 1986; Wiener, 1985, 1987; Wiener & Kohler, 1986). *Psychological Abstracts* (a major indexing system for psychological research), for example, does not have a reference or key word for reports. If you want to find research on reports in *Psychological Abstracts*, you must look under various general topics, such as psychometrics or school, clinical, or counseling psychology. In sum, while psychologists have continued to write reports of psychological evaluations, they have not nearly as often investigated reporting practices themselves.

An informal review of colleagues' training experiences suggests that most psychologists learn about report writing only as a peripheral part of their training in assessment and that they are rarely specifically taught how to write reports. During graduate training, psychologists are preoccupied with learning the mechanics of test administration and scoring and spend little time reflecting on how to write the assessment report. Instructors teach students how to write reports only as a secondary, or even unimportant, part of assessment courses. Worse, the same instructors rarely have a guide with which to teach students about report writing, a skill specific to psychology although it necessarily draws on the writer's previous education. Even after formal training in assessment techniques is completed, the demands of everyday practice may make psychologists reluctant to spend the time needed to examine their reporting practices critically. As you will see in subsequent chapters, taking time to reflect on your writing and to obtain feedback from your readers may be essential to improving your reports.

Psychologists often find report writing an onerous task, to be undertaken only under duress. There are many reasons why psychologists don't like to write reports. Most authors would agree that writing well is difficult, and writing reports certainly involves the skill of writing. There are also a number of reasons why writing well is difficult; one arises from the unavoidable fact that English is not written in the same way that it is spoken. Competent speakers of English are not always competent writers, and most of us know that if we simply write down exactly what we say, the result is likely to be unintelligible. This highlights the fact that translating ideas that may be well expressed in conversations with clients, parents, and colleagues into written English can be a stumbling block.

Introduction

Even when psychologists are competent at translating ideas into writing, another problem remains. Report writing remains a skill that, like any other, must be practiced and reflected upon to be mastered and maintained. Reports don't always improve with experience because little is learned when a report is assembled hastily for the typist without taking time for reflection on its content and organization. We simply tend to repeat the same mistakes over and over again when the process of writing reports becomes automatic. For these reasons, psychologists can feel frustrated with report writing and avoid it. If, in addition, they do not have a systematic method for putting their ideas into writing or concrete guidelines for ways to improve their reports, the task may be frustrating and even at times overwhelming.

This book addresses these issues in several ways. First, a theory-based outline of report writing problems is developed later in this introduction. The outline provides a structure for understanding exactly what problems are implicit in report writing and how they may be approached. Second, a survey of research and expert opinion on reporting is made in Chapter 1 to determine whether there already are solutions to the problems raised in the outline. You probably will note that most of the important issues in reporting have not been researched adequately and that often guidance must be drawn from a consensus of what other authors have recommended about the structure, organization, and content of report.

Later in this book, several lines of research are synthesized into a concrete model with a specific method for writing sentences and paragraphs in reports. Along the way, some of the differences between spoken and written English are discussed in order to clarify the process of transforming ideas about the assessment into comprehensible written statements. The ideas that underlie the model also provide guidance on techniques for moving from raw assessment data to relevant statements about the persons assessed. These are explained and illustrated, and ways of organizing statements into larger sections in the report are presented. Final chapters of the book review ways of tailoring reports to their use in specific contexts and across psychological specialties. Throughout, material for illustration and practice has been provided. Appendices A, B, and C provide illustrative material for learning the model and for diagnosing your reports, and Appendix D includes a number of reports as examples of the principles discussed elsewhere.

Although this book will not make you a master of psychological report writing overnight, the model and procedures described can help you at the outset to define the reporting task better. Use of the model and procedures over time also should help you to develop better reporting skills by encouraging you to reflect on how you write, to obtain feedback from your readers, and to tailor the reports you write to the contexts in which they will be used. The model reports in Appendix D and the practice material in Appendices A and B can help you master better the points reviewed. Before we turn to these topics, though, the theory of reporting, including the outline of important issues, should be discussed.

The Theory of Psychological Report Writing

At first glance, psychological report writing may not seem worthy of its own theory. It may appear that an attempt to create a theory of reporting is to take the task too seriously, to make something that is obvious and simple excessively formal. The subject thus might seem trivial and serious discussion therefore unnecessary.

Research on reports shows, however, that consumers of reports often are dissatisfied with our product. If their comments are used to gauge how well reports are written, then many reports do not communicate assessment results adequately. At best, reports often are viewed as inadequate; at worst, they are seen as serving unintentionally malicious purposes. Some research evidence has shown that reports can have a positive effect on how teachers, for example, view their competence in working with children. This suggests that if reports can have positive effects, they also can have negative ones. Therefore, psychologists must be careful to write reports that do not harm inadvertently. A theory of reporting can help psychologists write reports that are most likely to be helpful and least likely to be harmful.

Because few researchers have approached the same questions in ways that allow comparisons of their findings, it also seems likely that investigative efforts might profitably be coordinated within the structure of a theory. With a theory of report writing, then, researchers would better be able to identify relevant research questions. Results of current investigations then might be related more easily to those of previous studies, and future studies can be generated more readily.

Working from previous research and opinion on reporting practices, it has been possible to develop a theory of report writing. The ideas that it incorporates allow explicit consideration of variables crucial in writing effective reports. Among these are internal variables, such as style, content, and format, as well as external variables, such as for whom the report is written and the purpose for which it is sent. The theory consists of a set of basic concepts and related ideas that, organized in outline structure, detail the most important issues in report writing. The outline can, in turn, be used also by those interested in research to generate testable hypotheses about reports. The major headings in the outline are comprehensive, and it can be used to coordinate results of other studies. What follows is an explanation of the theory's basic ideas. They will be used in organizing most of the remainder of this book.

Basic Idea One: *The main purpose of psychological reports is to communicate information about a client to the reader in a way that will result in changes in the reader's beliefs about or behavior toward the client.* Although the words "main purpose" allow that reports may function in other ways—such as providing a written record of the assessment for future review—the primary reason for writing a report is to persuade someone to believe or to do something that the psychologist thinks will benefit the client. A critical implication of this concept is that reports should contain statements that are viewed as credible (belief-changing) or persuasive (behavior-changing) by their readers. This implication has been used to generate several tests of the model, which will be discussed further below (Ownby, 1990a, 1990b; see Chapter 2).

Basic Idea Two: *Reports can be analyzed according to their structure and content.* The word "structure" is used broadly here to include the ways in which the elements of sentences, paragraphs, sections, and the entire report are put together. "Content" here refers only to general categories of possible report content, such as test data vs. behavioral observations or information about clients' cognitive or emotional function. Although it may seem obvious that such analyses are possible, this idea is essential to the development of research strategies. Following from this is the possibility that investigations of structure and content will allow writers to specify which structures and contents will be most credible or persuasive.

Basic Idea Three: *How reports are organized can be evaluated.* Again, this may seem obvious, but this idea is a necessary preliminary to further study. Here, the word "organized" refers to the various models (domain- or hypothesis-oriented), formats (letter, brief narrative, lengthy narrative), and writing styles (informal or formal) that can be used in writing reports. An implication of this idea is that research studies can be conducted in such a manner that the best ways to organize reports can be determined.

Basic Idea Four: *How reports function in contexts can be evaluated.* An implication here is that even though relevant contextual variables are numerous and their interactions complex, it is possible to reduce this complexity to a level that allows empirical investigation. One way in which this might be accomplished, for example, would be by establishing broad categories of contextual variables. Contextual variables might include the reasons that underlie the initial request for assessment, the types of settings to which the report will be sent, and the number of persons from different professions who will see the report (Ownby, 1986b; Ownby, Wallbrown, & D'Atri, 1984; Ownby, Wallbrown, D'Atri, & Armstrong, 1985).

Basic Idea Five: *Variables important for understanding report writing can be organized in a framework of categories.* This basic idea simply serves as the justification for the structure of the outline. Three major categories of reporting variables are included in the outline: (a) structural, (b) organizational, and (c) contextual. These can be defined:

Structural. These are internal variables that have to do with the ways in which the basic elements of sentences, paragraphs, and sections of the report are put together. The expository process model described in Chapter 3 gives guidelines for dealing with structural issues by specifying how raw assessment data, theoretical constructs, conclusions, and recommendations should be organized. There are only a few studies on structural variables in psychological report writing (for example, Ownby, 1984, 1990a,

1990b); they have shown that the model may be useful in writing sentences and paragraphs in reports.

The theory predicts that these variables shouldn't change even though they are evaluated within different report organizations and in different settings. Research that addresses the best type of sentence structure in a report, for example, should be applicable whatever report organization scheme is used in whatever environment. Research has tentatively supported this prediction (Ownby, 1984, 1990a, 1990b). This invariance is in marked contrast to the other two categories of factors, which interact with each other to a great degree.

Organizational. These are also internal variables, but define how sentences, paragraphs, and sections are organized in the report. These include model, format, and style, all of which involve issues of high-level report organization rather than the basic structure of sentences and paragraphs. They probably vary interactively with contextual variables, so that, for example, the organization of a report written for the purpose of helping a public school teacher better understand one of his or her students is different from the report written to a private practice physician who has requested an evaluation of a patient in order to find out what part stress plays in the patient's illness.

Contextual. These variables are external to the report itself and have to do with the ways in which the report is affected by its context. These factors — referral agent, problem, and environment — vary across contexts and influence the basic organization of the report. The referral agent can vary by profession, level of training, and openness of agenda in making the referral for evaluation. The referral problem varies by type of problem, and the referral environment varies in complexity. All these factors should be considered in choosing a report's model, format, and style.

Basic Idea Six: *The effects of structural variables are invariant across contexts.* This implies that the best type of sentence, paragraph, or section is the same whether the report is written by a clinical, counseling, or school psychologist for another psychologist, a physician, or an attorney. A corollary of this postulate is that, through research, the best way of dealing with structural variables can be defined. This corollary thus holds the promise that even though reports must be tailored to their contexts, it may be possible to define certain invariants across situations so that every report does not have to be written as a completely new entity. For example, if it were found that reports should probably be written with a particular sentence structure and should include particular types of content, your work load could be reduced considerably. As noted, this idea has received some support from research.

Basic Idea Seven: *The effects of organizational variables vary across contextual variables.* This idea states that, in contrast to structural issues, report factors such as model, format, and style should vary according to the characteristics of the referral agent, problem, and environment. This implies that a report written to another psychologist to be read only by him or her should be different from the report written to a public school teacher that also might be read by the school counselor or building administrator. An important corollary is that reports are most likely to be effective when their organizations are allowed to vary in ways consistent with their contexts. An implication is that no one type of report will be best in all contexts. A second implication is that the writer of reports should be flexible in his or her approach to reporting, assessing contextual variables and modifying report organization as a result.

These seven basic ideas and their subordinate related concepts allow construction of a comprehensive outline of reporting variables (Figure 1). The outline, in turn, provides a means for identifying testable research areas and for making predictions about the probable results of research efforts. We will return to this outline in Chapter 8. The following example illustrates the potential usefulness of the outline by showing how it can organize hypotheses about report writing, which then can be tested in research studies.

The theory of report writing states that the effects of structural variables in reports are invariant across contexts or settings. The expository process model recommends specific structures for writing sentences and paragraphs (Ownby & Wallbrown, 1986). The model also states that certain elements should be included in a particular order in each statement and predicts that the same structure should

FIGURE 1
COMPREHENSIVE OUTLINE FOR REPORTING VARIABLES

I. <u>Structural Variables</u>
  A. *Sentences*
    1. Sequence of elements
    2. Content of elements
  B. *Paragraphs*
    1. Sequence of elements
    2. Content of elements
  C. *Sections*
    1. Sequence of elements
    2. Content of elements

II. <u>Organizational Variables</u>
  A. *Models*
    1. Hypothesis-oriented
    2. Domain-oriented
    3. Test-oriented
  B. *Formats*
    1. Letter
    2. Brief narrative
    3. Lengthy narrative
    4. Recommendations only
  C. *Style*
    1. Formality
    2. Vocabulary choice
    3. Grammatic structure

III. <u>Contextual Variables</u>
  A. *Referral Agent*
    1. Profession
    2. Level of training
    3. Agenda
    4. Familiarity with writer
  B. *Referral Problem*
    1. Type of problem
    2. Clarity of problem
  C. *Referral Environment*
    1. Primary vs. secondary readers
    2. Diversity of professions of readers

be effective in all contexts. By operationalizing the structural variables and making a theory-based prediction, a test of the theory becomes possible. Research results to date support the theory's contention that structural variables are invariant across contextual variables. Model-based statements consistently have been rated as more credible and persuasive across contextual variables, including profession (psychologist, counselor, and social worker) and work setting (school, community mental health center, university, and state psychiatric hospital; Ownby, 1984, 1990a, 1990b). Thus, these results provide support for the theory.

The Practice of Psychological Report Writing

Kurt Lewin said, "There is nothing so practical as a good theory" (in Marrow, 1969, p. viii). Lewin clearly understood the multiple roles that a theory can play in influencing practice. Although there may be intrinsic value in developing a theory of reporting, its most important function is to guide report writers whose reports may have significant impacts on clients' welfare. This guidance function is particularly important because many questions about report writings have not been addressed by researchers. A theory that is consistent with empirical research can predict what ought to be true in other unresearched situations. Even though tests of a given prediction are unavailable, at least we can proceed with a reasoned approach to the problems inherent in reporting the results of psychological assessments.

The rest of this book deals with the problems that arise in the practice of reporting individual psychological assessments. Throughout the discussion, it will be helpful to keep in mind the outline presented above so that you can relate it to the questions discussed. In the final chapter, the outline is reviewed and reconsidered in light of the evidence presented in the book.

2

RESEARCH ON REPORTS

To date, there has been relatively little research on what makes psychological reports effective, although researchers recently have shown more interest in this topic. Therefore, much of any review of reporting must consist of expert opinion about reports rather than of research efforts aimed at an empirical understanding of them. In this chapter, some of the relevant literature on report writing is reviewed in order to provide a better understanding of common problems. Although it is not exhaustive, this review includes many important references on report writing that illustrate both past and current research and problems. When appropriate, additional references are cited in later chapters to illustrate important points.

The aim of this review is to survey research on reports so that typical problems can be identified and solutions offered. A subordinate aim is to identify and make explicit what purposes psychological reports should serve, so that better evaluation criteria can be formulated. When research findings are not available, opinions expressed by appropriate authorities are surveyed in order to determine whether there is a consensus on the issue in question. When no consensus can be reached, the best guess that can be made is offered.

Work has continued on a research program targeted at determining precisely what it is that makes a report effective and at defining relevant referral and context variables. For example, my colleagues and I have researched the characteristics of reports received by special education teachers (Ownby, Wallbrown, & Brown, 1982), proposed that using a questionnaire to obtain feedback about report can be useful in improving them (Ownby & Wallbrown, 1983), and developed a classification system for child referral problems that allows specification of the type of report most likely to be useful with particular referral problems. (See Chapter 5; Ownby et al., 1984; Ownby et al., 1985; Westman, Ownby, & Smith, 1987.) We also have developed a model for writing reports based on the report writing research and on a psycholinguistic model of discourse comprehension (Ownby, 1984, 1990a, 1990b; Ownby & Wallbrown, 1986).

We hope that this program will supply needed information about reporting practices. In the meantime, research findings and authorities' opinions can be considered and a consensus, when possible, drawn from them. Although it would be logical to organize the following review based on the sections of the comprehensive outline presented in the introduction, it has not been possible to take this approach. Most studies to be reviewed here did not focus explicitly on just one of the variables in the outline; most can be interpreted as addressing several divergent variables. The following review has therefore been organized around broad topical clusters, which consist of the settings in which the research took place or the general issue with which the research was concerned.

Research in Clinical Settings

Research has shown that psychological reports in clinical settings are (a) sometimes considered useful by persons who receive the reports, such as psychiatrists and social workers; (b) frequently criticized by these professional groups on both content and stylistic grounds; and (c) may (or may not) make substantial contributions to client treatment planning.

In an early study, Garfield, Heine, and Leventhal (1954) studied views of psychological reports among three professional groups (psychologists, psychiatrists, and social workers) in a clinic setting. Psychiatrists criticized reports for the inclusion of excessive speculation, for failure to include data from which inferences were drawn, and for vagueness and ambiguity in writing style. In the same study, psychologists also criticized the reports for failing to include the behavioral data from which inferences were drawn and for stylistic problems that included vagueness and the use of jargon. Social workers as a group were least critical of reports.

Cuadra and Albaugh (1956) studied the relation between what authors intended to write in reports and the message the reports' readers received. As they found at best a modest agreement between intended and received messages, Cuadra and Albaugh encourage psychologists to be careful to make their messages explicit in reports.

In a classic study of reports, Tallent and Reiss (1959a, 1959b, 1959c) compared three professional groups' opinions of report contents and found that psychologists, psychiatrists, and social workers showed many common interests in the content of reports, as well as important differences. For example, while all three groups indicated that a general personality description and a discussion of dynamic defenses, interpersonal relations, and intellectual status were appropriate content, differences appeared on a few related issues. One area of divergence was on the issue of reporting IQ test results: "The psychiatrists and social workers appear to be more interested in having a statement of IQ or intelligence level than the psychologists are in reporting it" (1959a, p. 218, 221). In addition, while 74% of the psychologists indicated that recommendations for treatment were an appropriate content of reports, only 14% of the psychiatrists expressed this view. It appears that the psychologists were more interested in giving an opinion than the psychiatrists were in receiving it.

Perhaps the most interesting result of Tallent and Reiss's study came from a sentence completion item included in their survey, the stem of which was, "The trouble with psychological reports is. . ." Tallent and Reiss obtained responses to this stem from a total of 712 psychologists, psychiatrists, and psychiatric social workers. The principal complaints voiced by these professionals included "irresponsible interpretation" of data and "expressive deficiencies" (1959c, p. 446). "Irresponsible interpretation" in general referred to over- or underinterpretation of data or to statements that appeared to reflect the examiner's personality more than the client's. "Expressive deficiencies" referred to the use of jargon, to wordiness, and to ambiguity of content.

In a later study, Lacey and Ross (1964) examined attitudes of three professional groups toward psychological reports in child guidance clinics, they found both similarities and differences between their results and those of Tallent and Reiss. Data were reported for a total of 150 psychologists, psychiatrists, and social workers in 10 child guidance clinics. One similarity between Lacey and Ross's results and Tallent and Reiss's was that workers in both settings believed that information about the appearance and behavior of the client during assessment should be included in the report. An interesting difference between the two studies was that a larger percentage of professionals in the Lacey and Ross study felt that recommendations that concerned client treatment should be included in the report. Another important difference between the two studies concerned the willingness of psychologists to include raw assessment data in the report (such as responses to projective test stimuli or observations of patient behavior during testing). Here, the psychologists in the child guidance setting were more willing to include these types of data in their reports. Lacey and Ross interpret this finding as showing that reports might be written differently depending on relations between professional groups in varying settings. Finally, all three professional groups in this study reported much less dissatisfaction with expressive variables than was found by Tallent and Reiss.

Hartlage, Freeman, Horine, and Walton (1968) used a different research strategy to determine the usefulness of statements frequently found in reports to psychiatrists who were making decisions with regard to clients. Hartlage et al. found a correlation of −.50 between a panel of psychiatrists' ratings of the usefulness of statements abstracted from a large number of reports and the frequency of these statements' appearance in reports. While this procedure does not indicate that the reports that contained the statements were not useful, by inference frequent statements might be expected to show at least a modest positive relation to rated usefulness. Hartlage et al. (1968) conclude that "it appears that this sample of psychological reports was evidently of little value in contributing toward any treatment decisions for the patients" (p. 483).

Moore, Boblitt, and Wildman (1968) surveyed a sample of psychiatrists in one institution, as well as a random sample of psychiatrists in the southeastern United States. They found that the majority of psychiatrists did not view psychological assessment as

an essential part of client evaluation and that it "would not be used in any additional case planning even if changes were made in the structure of the report to make it more desirable" (p. 373). Among those psychiatrists who regularly used psychological evaluations as part of their treatment, however, Moore et al. (1968) found that they would like the report to present a more detailed evaluation of client motivations, an outline of the client's problems, and suggestions about how to deal with them.

In another research study, Lacks, Horton, and Owen (1969) compared psychiatrists' satisfaction with a checklist report, a written outline report, and the standard narrative report. They found that many psychiatrists believe that standard psychological reports contain "too much irrelevant or needless information" and are often "too long, redundant, subjective, and over general" (p. 386). On the other hand, the information provided by the checklist alone was described as too limited. The written outline format received favorable ratings from psychiatrists, and the authors conclude that it might be used in settings in which there is pressure for prompt reporting of assessment data.

Affleck and Strider (1971) investigated the use of psychological reports in the development of client treatment plans in a psychiatric facility which provided both in- and outpatient services to children and adults. A total of 340 referral requests and reports and the reports' subsequent effects on treatment plans were investigated. In this study, persons who made referrals (usually psychiatric residents) were encouraged to indicate the types of information desired and to make specific referral requests. The authors conclude that the psychiatrists were provided with useful information, as "there is indication that 52% of the reports actually altered management in some direct way" (p. 179). These results contrast with other negative evaluations of the usefulness of reports. Here, it should be noted that the person who made the referral was asked to make specific information requests and to state the referral question clearly. This practice may have influenced the usefulness or relevance of the information obtained during the assessment by helping the psychologists give the psychiatrists the information they needed for client treatment.

More recently, several authors have commented on the function of evaluating clients as part of determining their eligibility for

disability benefits and the role that reports may play in this process. Although these were not empirical studies of report writing, they are reviewed briefly here because of their relevance to report writing in clinical settings. Binder (1987) discusses the specific issue of the manner in which Wechsler Adult Intelligence Scale – Revised (WAIS-R) IQ and subtest scores should be reported. Binder notes that reporting age-corrected score with older clients may be misleading if their performances are to be compared with those of younger persons. He argues for the use of non-age-corrected scores in such comparisons. This is a clinical setting example of the need to change reporting practices when the purpose of the evaluation varies because of its context.

Kodimer (1988) discusses report writing in disability determinations more extensively. He suggests that one important reason for denial of disability benefits is inadequate reporting of assessment results. Kodimer reviews Social Security Administration guidelines for disability determination and then overviews ways of tailoring reports to communicate critical information most effectively. Kodimer proposes a number of specific issues that should be dealt with in such a report, such as the client's capacity for carrying out tasks of independent daily living, maintaining satisfactory interpersonal relations, and focusing attention in a sustained fashion. Reporting on these points, Kodimer asserts, will facilitate a review of the client's claim by Social Security. An inference to be drawn here is that, once again, it is important to tailor the report within its context.

Research in School Settings

The lack of research on the impact of psychological reports in school settings is especially disconcerting given the intense scrutiny that special education placement procedures have received in recent years, at least in part because of the advent of Public Law 94–142. This law mandates safeguards in the evaluation and programming of children with special educational needs, areas in which school psychologists often are involved. Several authors have suggested that special educators may be dissatisfied with aspects of school psychological services in general and with reports in particular (Gaddes, 1983; Keogh, 1972; Ownby, 1982; Ownby et al., 1982). Much research on school psychological reports has investigated

teacher satisfaction with reports, although a more recent focus has been on determining how information from reports influences teacher attitudes and behaviors.

An early study by Mussman (1964) of teacher satisfaction with reports used twelve teachers as judges to evaluate a procedure in which they were given a brief handwritten report immediately after completion of the assessment. The traditional reports were forwarded to the teacher several weeks later in accordance with usual school system procedures. Evaluations of this process indicated that teachers preferred the immediate feedback report, but also valued the traditional report for its more extensive information and recommendations. Teachers stated that the reports could be improved by including observations of the child's behavior during assessment and by making the recommendations section of the report larger and more concrete.

Baker (1965) provided data about reports drawn from a broader investigation of the perceptions of teachers, counselors, and administrators of psychological services in schools. In contrast to the negative findings of some studies, Baker reports that "the claim that the reports of the school psychologists are commonly too technical, theoretical, or are written in a vague style, was not substantiated in this study. Teachers and counselors found information to be conveyed in a relatively coherent manner" (p. 39). An interesting and possibly significant finding of this study stems from Baker's comparison of the extent to which reports were useful to inexperienced teachers (less than four years of teaching) and experienced teachers (more than four years). Although "roughly half" (p. 39) of the inexperienced teachers responded that the report had added to their knowledge of the problem, only 28% of the experienced teachers made this response. This pattern shows that school psychologists may play a more important role in helping inexperienced teachers deal with student problems than in helping more experienced faculty.

Rucker (1967a) reported an investigation of teacher ratings of the usefulness of reports written by experienced vs. less experienced psychologists and by psychologists with classroom teaching experience vs. those without this experience. All comparisons among these groups were statistically nonsignificant, but the four elementary school teachers who served as judges contributed several valuable comments on the characteristics of useful reports. As a rule, the judges in Rucker's study stated that the more useful reports answered the referral questions clearly and "presented a well-rounded program consisting of a variety of specific recommendations to aid the teacher" (p. 105). Rucker also observes that the recommendations judged most helpful by the teachers were those that showed that the writer understood how the recommendations might be implemented in the classroom.

In a second study, Rucker (1967b) investigated the degree to which commonly used terms in psychological reports represent meaningful communication rather than jargon to teachers, by comparing agreement between groups of psychologists and elementary school teachers on the meanings of frequently used terms. Rucker's findings showed that even psychologists disagreed among themselves on definitions of some terms and that there were even greater disagreements between psychologists and teachers. Rucker concludes that psychologists should use fewer technical terms and write reports in language which is likely to be clear to the report's intended recipient.

Brandt and Giebink (1968) studied ways in which the concreteness of recommendations and the congruence of interpretations of child behavior with teacher attitudes affect teacher preferences for reports. They found that teachers preferred reports whose interpretations indicated an accepting attitude toward the child regardless of whether such an attitude was congruent with their own. Brandt and Giebink conclude that their results support others' emphases on the need for providing specific recommendations in reports.

A study by Shively and Smith (1969) examined the extent to which teachers, counselors, and undergraduate teacher-education students understood terms frequently used in reports. Their findings indicate that although counselors understood more of the technical terms drawn from a sample of reports than did the other two groups, only 54% of the technical terms were understood overall.

Noting "a surprising lack of published material which documents the effectiveness of the practice of preparing diagnostic reports," Waugh (1970, p. 631) reports an investigation of the issue. Graduate students at a university learning-disabilities clinic prepared reports after they had worked with children for 25 hours over an eight-week period. The reports were given to each child's classroom teacher, and two weeks later a questionnaire was sent to the teachers. Waugh found that 61% of the reports were rated as useful in planning for the child, but only 23 questionnaires were returned. Waugh concludes from her study that "emphasis on educational deficits does improve the impact of the psycho-diagnostic reports" (p. 632). It must be noted, however, that Waugh draws this conclusion from a comparison of her results with those of the study by Baker (discussed above), which showed that half of the inexperienced teachers and slightly more than a fourth of the experienced teachers in Baker's sample found that reports contributed to their understanding of the child assessed. Waugh's conclusion is questionable in light of the small number of questionnaires returned, the fact that the questions asked of the respondents were not the same, and the possible differences between the two groups of teachers.

In a dissertation study, Sudduth (1976) investigated the effects of three methods of reporting assessment data to teachers. After an assessment was completed, teachers received one of four combinations of report and consultation: (a) written report only; (b) face-to-face consultation only; (c) report and consultation; or (d) no report or consultation. The report and consultation group showed significant increases in teacher-psychologist agreement about the nature of the problem, but no other significant treatment effects were observed. This finding supports the idea that the report in conjunction with consultation is an important part of providing school psychological services.

Also in a dissertation study, Littlejohn (1977) compared preferences for three report formats among school psychologists, elementary teachers, elementary principals, and educators of school psychologists. Formats studied were (a) traditional narrative; (b) brief checklist; and (c) brief narrative with emphasis on recommendations. A central finding was that all groups showed the strongest preference for the traditional narrative format. Littlejohn also asked participants to rank the sections of the report in order of importance. All groups ranked the recommendations section as most useful.

Isett and Roszkowski (1979) studied the value of various sections of the report to workers in a short-term residential facility for mentally retarded persons. They found that the reports' users believed that recommendations and information about the clients' social competence were most valuable and that projective test data and IQ test results were least valuable in their work with these clients.

Bagnato (1980) examined differences between two styles of writing diagnostic reports. A group of 48 teachers in early childhood handicapped education programs received training in developing curricular objectives from assessment data. They then were asked to develop educational programs for students either from traditional psychological reports or from "translated" reports whose recommendations were keyed to specific developmental curriculum goals. Bagnato found that the "translated" reports were superior to the traditional reports in helping teachers to develop educational programs. Bagnato makes the following recommendations about reports: (a) they should be organized by ability domain rather than by test; (b) they should describe strengths and weaknesses in behavioral terms; (c) they should emphasize process variables, such as learning strategies; (d) they should link assessment tasks closely to curricular goals in order to facilitate educational plan development; and (e) they should provide teachers with recommendations for behavioral management techniques.

In a study of how teachers view reports from clinical psychologists, Berry (1975) found that even though about 30% of the same believed that there was too much psychological terminology in reports and that the reports were neither clear nor lucid, 65% were generally satisfied with the reports they had received. Of additional interest are Berry's findings that 86% of the teachers wanted the report to help in making decisions about the child and that 61% rated the specific recommendations sections as the most useful part of the report in working with the child. The return rate of Berry's questionnaire, however, was a low 46%.

Finally, Ownby et al. (1982) investigated special education teachers' perceptions of reports. They found that important components of each section of the report (for example, observations of a child's behavior in the classroom or a discussion of his or her social-emotional status) were included with varying frequencies in reports received by the teachers. This finding suggests that important report elements sometimes were omitted. They also found that reports received by these teachers often did not include a statement of the test results' validity, in contrast to the recommendation by a number of authorities that such a statement be included. Another finding was that while behavioral observations often were included in reports, the behaviors observed rarely were linked to antecedent behaviors. This suggests that although psychologists may have believed that child behavior was important, they did not systematically assess it in order to design strategies for changing it.

In more recent years, studies have in general begun to focus more closely on specific issues about reporting that are amenable to empirical investigation. This trend represents a transition from studies that merely documented consumers' dissatisfaction with reports to attempts to study reporting variables and their effects on the process of communication with readers. For example, Witt, Moe, Gutkin, and Andrews (1984) studied the effects of different types of jargon on the acceptability to teachers of potential classroom interventions for behavior problems. They developed essentially identical interventions for both mild and severe behavior problems and couched them in either behavioristic, humanistic, or pragmatic (e.g., logical consequences) terms. They found that interventions phrased pragmatically (e.g., staying in from recess for not completing work) were rated more acceptable than the same interventions phrased in the other two sets of terms.

Weddig (1984) reviewed 50 psychological reports and determined their reading levels. She then drew one report from the sample that had a median reading difficulty and made it more readable by changing vocabulary, replacing professional terminology with behavioral descriptions, and removing irrelevant information. Parents then were asked to read either the original report or its modification and then were tested for their comprehension of the content. Weddig concludes that her modifications made the report more understandable for the parents and recommends that psychologists use readability measures in evaluating their reports. She also makes the specific recommendations that psychologists should write reports at a lower level of reading difficulty, should replace professional terms with descriptions of behaviors, and should remove content not related to the placement decision.

Wiener, in a series of studies (1985, 1987; Wiener & Kohler, 1986), has worked to define variables related to consumers' satisfaction with and comprehension of psychological reports. Consistent with results of other studies, Wiener found that teachers understood reports better that organized information according to ability areas, described strengths and weaknesses in behavioral terms rather than jargon, and clearly explained recommendations (Wiener, 1985). In this study, Wiener also found that teachers preferred reports that explicitly responded to the referral questions. In other studies, Wiener found similar results with groups of parents and with groups of other educators (Wiener, 1985; Wiener & Kohler, 1986). This series of studies is particularly important because they studied not only consumer preferences, but also consumers' understanding of the information conveyed by the report. These studies confirm the relation between consumer preference and consumer ability to acquire desired information.

Biasing Information in Reports

An important area of recent research on report writing deals with the effects of biasing information in reports on teachers' perceptions of and behaviors toward children. Usually, these studies bear most directly on school psychological reports, but they are relevant to report writing in other specialties as well. Interest in this area perhaps was sparked by Rosenthal and Jacobson's (1968) pioneering work, which showed that teacher expectations based on information about children's abilities may have an impact on the same children's eventual classroom success. While these studies bypass the as yet unresolved issue of whether reports do, in fact, affect teachers' behaviors, the significant effects of biasing information on teachers' beliefs suggest that reports are influential in attitude change. However, studies that have examined this issue have not shown consistently that reports have significant impacts on teachers' attitudes or behaviors.

Robinson (1974) studied the effects of two methods of psychological service delivery on children's group achievement test performance. This research was somewhat artificial in that the children involved were not referred for problems, but were chosen from all children in a school system's third-grade class. The 39 children selected were administered a standard battery of tests. In one treatment condition, teachers received a test report written in jargon and did not have a conference with the psychologist, while in a second condition test results were reported in a conference and a clearly written report included detailed recommendations. Even with such extreme differences in service delivery, children's group achievement test scores did not vary significantly between conditions after three months. Further, teachers' ratings of the children's improvement in scholastic abilities did not vary either.

In an investigation that suggests that reports may influence teachers' perceptions of students, Mertens (1976) studied the effects of biased reports on teachers' ratings of student essays. A group of 94 teachers in training were given biased reports about a hypothetical child. They were then asked to rate an essay by the child and fill out a report card on the child according to their expectations for the child's achievement at the end of the school year. Results showed that biasing information in reports can influence teacher perceptions of student performance (ratings of the essay) and their expectations for student success (estimated end-of-year grades).

Schwartz (1977) showed that certain types of information in reports may differentially influence teachers' perceptions of children. Schwartz provided either information about what to do with a child who was exhibiting problems ("Type I") or explanatory information about why the child functioned in the manner described ("Type II"). This study showed that Type I information positively changed teachers' perceptions of the child's ability to improve, of the child's potential to be disruptive, and of the teachers' ability to deal with the child's difficulties in the classroom. Type II information positively changed teachers' perceptions of the child's degree of exceptionality and their emotional reactions to the child.

Schwartz and Wilkinson (1987) studied the effects of diagnostic labels provided in mocked-up school folders on teachers' reactions to report contents. They found that diagnostic labels affected how teachers interpreted data in reports (even when the data contradicted the proposed diagnostic label) and conclude, "teachers' perceptions of various types of exceptional children are differentially affected by the unique combinations of prior expectation, report data and interpretation, and the specific kinds of academic and social/emotional behavior under consideration" (p. 134).

These studies show that information provided in psychological reports has the potential to affect teachers' perceptions of and expectations for students. The nature of these effects is clearly complex—Schwartz's study, for example, has shown that type of information may interact with type of attitude or belief change obtained. The relations between information, expectations, and teacher behavior are still more complex, as is suggested by Robinson's failure to find a significant impact of report information on children's academic achievement test scores. Mertens' results, however, are consistent with the idea that the favorability of information provided to teachers may influence their expectations for student performance.

As a group, these studies show that reports may have an important impact on teacher perceptions and expectations, but a clear conclusion about the nature of this impact and its ultimate meaning for teacher behavior cannot be drawn. In all specialties, it is probably prudent to include information in the report about both the client's strengths and weaknesses, to explain why the client functions as he or she does, and to provide specific recommendations (when desired by the referring agent) about how to work with the client.

Barnum Effect

An important area of research in test interpretation and reporting concerns the Barnum effect. This effect arises from the observation that personality interpretations that are sufficiently vague are true of most persons (Dana & Fouke, 1979; Forer, 1949; O'Dell, 1972; M. Smith, 1986; Sundberg, 1955). Dickson and Kelly provide examples of several categories of Barnum statements. Some are vague, such as, "you enjoy a certain amount of change and variety in life;" some are "double-headed," such as "you are generally cheerful and optimistic but get depressed at times;" some describe "modal characteristics of the subject's group," such as "you find that study is not always easy;" and some are frankly positive, such as "you are forceful and well-liked by others" (1985, p. 367).

Although few, if any, studies have demonstrated that Barnum statements are a significant problem in reports that actually are used in practice, it is apparent that such statements could be incorporated easily into reports and uncritically accepted by readers. The result would be reports that are speciously acceptable to readers and give writers a false sense of having communicated something important about the client. The problem of the Barnum effect is discussed more fully in Chapters 2 and 3, below.

Improving Reports

Several authors have discussed ways of improving reports. Hartlage and Merck (1971), for example, asked supervisors in a rehabilitation facility to rank 31 frequently occurring statements drawn from reports according to their usefulness in helping them plan for clients of the facility. Information about the usefulness of various statements to supervisors subsequently was made available to the same psychologists whose reports were used in creating the list of frequently occurring statements. Hartlage and Merck then chose 20 reports each from the four-month periods prior to and subsequent to the feedback and asked supervisors to rate them. Hartlage and Merck found a "clear and consistent" (p. 460) superiority of new vs. old reports and suggest that the change was due not to a shift in the types of data presented in the reports, but to the more valuable way in which data were presented to the supervisors. Hartlage and Merck state that "reports can be made more relevant to their prospective users merely by having the psychologists familiarize themselves with the uses to which their reports are to be applied" (p. 460). They conclude that psychologists ought "to evaluate their own reports in terms of what these reports contribute to the operation of their unique settings rather than to continue to grind out reports with good theoretical consistency but little decisional value" (p. 460).

Taking into account these findings as well as other report research, Ownby and Wallbrown (1983) argue for the importance of obtaining specific feedback about reports as a way of improving them. They present a brief evaluative questionnaire to accompany each report as a way of learning whether a report answers the referral question, provides useful information and recommendations, and whether any terms contained in the report were difficult for its recipient to understand. In light of the substantial effect that feedback can have on a report's effectiveness, such a procedure may provide report writers with critically important information with which to improve their reporting practices. Subsequently, this approach also is suggested by Sattler (1988) in the third edition of his text.

Weddig (1984), in a study discussed more extensively above, argues for the use of readability formulae in making reports more understandable. She suggests that reports should be written at lower levels of readability than they are at present. Pryzwansky and Hanania (1986) applied research on experts' problem-solving behavior (e.g., Sloves, Docherty, & Schneider, 1979) to the organization of psychological reports. They suggested that reports organized according to these principles, which require a sequence of activities in problem solving that move from abstract statement of the problem to particular solutions, might be preferred by report consumers. In contrast to the expected preference, however, Pryzwansky and Hanania (1986) found a strong preference for the traditional report organization. They conclude that "attempts to improve the quality of psychological reports by changing their organization may be analogous to fixing something that is not broken" (p. 139).

Purposes of Psychological Reports

Many authors have reviewed the purposes of psychological reports. This issue is critical because explicitly defining the reasons for writing reports is a necessary preliminary to evaluating the extent to which reports accomplish their goals. A definition of purpose also can provide guidance to writers in deciding how to write reports. What most authorities suggest about reports' purposes, however, appears to be based on clinical experience, theoretical orientation, or personal preference rather than on empirical research. Research on the purposes of reports might clarify, for example, the functions that reports serve in particular contexts. It is conceivable that one type of report might be shown to be useful in recording the results of an assessment for future use, another type might be shown to be useful in communicating technical data to other professionals, while yet another type might be most effective in changing readers' beliefs and behaviors. Research on the appropriate goals of report writing across contexts is not available, which makes it difficult to define these questions further. For example, in one of the few studies of content variables in reports, Sinclair and Alexson (1986) found that information about academic achievement was critical in psychoeducational reports, while information about medical background was unrelated to placement. This result shows that defining the purpose of reports is an important prerequisite to determining their effectiveness.

As has been necessary in other areas, the purpose of this review must be limited to defining a consensus among authorities. Central issues on which a consensus emerges are: (a) the report should be written with the needs of the referring person in mind; (b) reports should provide information that is relevant to work with the client, but that may not have been requested; (c) reports should communicate in a way that is appropriate to the report's intended recipient, and (d) reports should affect the way the reader works with the client.

Most authorities agree on the importance of considering the questions that the report is to answer. Sundberg and Tyler (1962), for example, state that "as he [or she] organizes the material into a report, the foremost guide the clinician has in mind is: What are the questions this report is to answer—the purpose of this assessment work?" (p. 228). They continue this discussion with remarks that note that the written report may include not only answers to questions posed in the original referral, but also new information discovered in the assessment process that may be useful to the report's recipients. This point of view is echoed by Huber (1961), who states that "the function of a report is to answer questions" (p. 1), as well as by Klopfer (1960), who suggests that the report should contain practical information that will help those who are working with the client to determine appropriate courses of action.

Another point on which experts agree is the importance of considering the context in which the report is to serve. Here, the purpose of the report is implicitly to communicate assessment information in a way that is easily comprehensible to the referring person. Harrower (1965), for example, suggests that the report writer should be thoroughly familiar with the context into which the report is sent. Appelbaum (1970) has gone further in suggesting that the problem with psychological reports lies not so much with the reports themselves, but with writers' failure to recognize their multiple roles in providing assessment information. Appelbaum argues that "the test report is part of a complex and dynamic social system" (p. 350) and that the psychologists' roles in this system include those of politician, diplomat, salesman, and artist, depending on the situations in which test data (whose purpose is to affect how others deal with clients) are communicated. Appelbaum's position, therefore, is that the purpose of reports is to communicate assessment information in a fashion appropriate to the intended reader so that the way the reader works with the client is affected. With respect to stylistic issues, Appelbaum recommends that the writer of the report strike a balance between the use of raw data and abstract statements, make appropriate use of technical language, and provide reasonable estimates of the confidence with which conclusions are drawn. He also suggests that the writer should try to make the report interesting to the reader.

Palmer's (1970) viewpoint on reports is illustrated by this statement: "It should be written to and for the referrant. It should reply clearly and succinctly to the referrant's questions" (p. 336). Palmer recognizes that the assessment also may produce data that are relevant to the treatment of the client, but not directly related to referral questions, and recommends that these data be included. Palmer does not explicitly comment on whether reports should attempt to affect work with clients, although it seems likely from the tone of the text that he would endorse this view.

In the first edition of his text on assessment of children, Sattler (1974) specifies three purposes of report writing: "To answer the referral question, to convey in as much depth as possible a meaningful description of the examinee, and to provide useful recommendations" (1974, p. 368). Sattler's view of the assessment procedure is thus somewhat broader than that of other authorities in that he makes explicit the idea that providing a description of the person assessed is itself also a legitimate goal of the report. In a more recent edition of this work, Sattler (1982, p. 510) summarizes his position again: "Psychological reports (a) provide a record of the child's performance; (b) communicate findings; (c) help in providing remediation suggestions; and (d) facilitate placement decisions." Thus, Sattler sees the psychological report as serving several purposes: recording, describing, and affecting work with clients.

In his comprehensive text on report writing, Tallent (1976) offers the following definition of a report, in it addressing the purpose of reports: "The psychological report may be defined as a document written as a means of understanding certain features about a person and his circumstances in order to make decisions about, for, or with him, and to intervene positively in his life" (p. 10). Thus, both Sattler and Tallent suggest that reports should serve multiple functions, and while Sattler proposes a somewhat wider range, Tallent emphasizes that the report should help to change something in the client's life. Shea (1985) argues that "the purpose of the report is to communicate *effectively* with the reader" (1985, pp. 7-8; emphasis in the original). Shea goes on to suggest that the report should function as an independent document that communicates "who the client is, why the assessment was performed, what was found, and what recommendations were proposed" (p. 8).

A review of these authorities' opinions indicates substantial consensus on certain aspects of reports' purposes. Nearly all authorities state, logically enough, that the report should respond directly to the questions of the referring agent. Nearly all also state that the report should provide data in a way that is appropriate to the understanding of the intended reader. Several authorities suggest that the report should provide a description of the client and a record of the psychologist's assessment activities. Virtually all the experts agree, either explicitly or implicitly, that the report should affect the way the report's recipient works with the client.

From these observations it is possible to offer a tentative statement on the purposes of psychological reports. The purposes of reports are:

1. to answer referral questions as explicitly as possible, depending on how well defined the questions are;
2. to provide the referring agent with additional information when it is relevant to his or her work with the client and when it is appropriate to the use to which the report will be put (this includes providing a general description of the client);
3. to make a record of the assessment activities for future use;
4. to recommend a specific course of action for which the recipient of the report to follow in his or her work with the client.

It should be clear that the overriding purpose of the psychological report should be to influence the way in which the report's reader deals with the client. Whether the report is answering questions, describing clients, or recording assessment data, the report should provide statements that alter the reader's beliefs about and behaviors toward clients. Thus, the report should provide statements that are *credible* (change beliefs) and *persuasive* (change behaviors). This is the definition of the purpose of reports used throughout the remainder of this book.

Literature on Reporting: Summary

The varied nature of the research on report writing reviewed here shows that few of the important issues about reporting have been researched adequately. As a result, it is not always possible to arrive at research–based decisions about how to write reports. Inferences can, however, be drawn from the review to provide tentative guidance about structural, content, organizational, and contextual variables. Thus, you can use research data and the consensus drawn from expert opinion to determine the most effective strategies for writing your reports. These inferences are sketched briefly in the remaining part of this chapter; subsequent chapters provide more complete discussions of how to implement the guidelines in your day-to-day practice. Issues discussed in the rest of this book include how to write sentences, paragraphs, and sections in the report, what material reports should contain, how they should be organized, and how they should be tailored to their contexts.

Writing. A review of problems in report writing suggests that writers do not always appreciate the importance of basic composition skills. Although a course in basic writing skills is beyond the scope of this book, a discussion of the relation of spoken English to written English may help you appreciate the importance of approaching writing as a special form of communication. Chapter 4 presents a discussion of this relation and provides an introduction to a psycholinguistic model for writing reports.

Structural variables. One of the few things that appears certain from review of the research on reporting is that reports often contain terms whose meanings are unclear to the reports' recipients. Nearly every author who has written about reports cautions writers not to use jargon. This suggestion appears especially important in light of findings such as Rucker's (1967b), which show that groups of typical report readers, and even psychologists themselves, disagree on the meanings of widely used terms. Virtually every writer who has commented on reports has argued against the use of technical vocabulary in reports, and many have suggested substitution of behavioral descriptions for this vocabulary. The importance of this issue also is highlighted by evidence that shows that even the type of jargon used can influence the acceptability of recommended interventions (Witt et al., 1984). It is clear that psychological terms should be used cautiously in reports both because they may be confusing to the reader and because they may affect his or her willingness to implement recommendations contained in the report.

A related problem stems from disagreement on the extent to which data such as behavior during testing should be included in the report. Research on readers' preferences shows that they want the writer to include some of the raw data upon which reports are based, but it is not clear how the writer is to select appropriate data and how he or she is to relate these data to conclusions and recommendations. The central task for the writer is to turn the raw data of the assessment into meaningful conclusions and recommendations. At some point in writing the report, he or she must decide how to move from basic data to more general statements about client function. It is at this point that many psychologists are likely to use terms that are not meaningful to the report's readers. The problem, then, may not be so much the terms themselves as their relation to other material in the report. These problems are addressed in the chapter on the Expository Process Model (Chapter 4).

Content variables. Issues within this area are both general and specific and range from a determination of the extent to which the report is to provide a broad picture of the client's functioning vs. answering only specific questions, to whether test scores should be included in the report. Studies that show the effects of biasing information suggest the importance of providing information about the client's strengths as well as the client's weaknesses. If information in the report only depicts a client with many problems and few resources for coping, the report reader may become pessimistic about the client's chances for improvement. Schwartz's (1977) finding that information about how to deal with a child may enhance teachers' belief in their ability to cope with the difficulties presented by the child underscores the need for a specific and detailed recommendations section in most reports. It also may be apparent that content issues cannot be separated arbitrarily from structural issues: the determination of how much and what sort of data to include in the report is at once an issue both of style and content. Content issues are discussed further in Chapter 7.

Organizational variables. It also is not easy to define the differences between organization and content. Many authorities (for example, Hollis & Donn, 1979; Klopfer, 1960; Tallent, 1976) have suggested formats for reports, and there is considerable agreement among authorities on the basic elements of these formats. It is also possible to deduce a report format based on a specification of reports' purposes. Chapter 7 on report organization addresses these concerns and shows how reports can be tailored to function within varying contexts and for various purposes.

Purposes of the report. Even in the basic area of deciding precisely what the report should do there is no obvious consensus. Most authors do, however, agree that the report should serve at least four purposes: (a) describing the client assessed and the client's problem; (b) recording the results of the evaluation for future use; (c) communicating the results of the assessment to interested persons; and (d) recommending an appropriate course of action. Several authors (Appelbaum, 1970; Tallent, 1976, 1980) argue that the report should serve what may be conveniently described as an influencing function in working to persuade the reader to alter his or her beliefs about the client and to undertake a particular course of action with respect to the client. These opinions allow the consensus that reports should affect the reader's beliefs and behaviors by providing statements which are credible and persuasive.

Referral problem. A critical problem in writing the report is to determine precisely what the referral question is and how to answer it as clearly as possible in a way suitable to the referring agent. One study already cited (Affleck & Strider, 1971) showed that a clear specification of the referral problem and an equally specific attempt to address it may make the report more useful in planning about the client. Ways of addressing this issue are discussed in Chapter 6.

Referral context. Both authorities and researchers strongly recommend that the writer consider the context of the report while writing it. Such a consideration of context will of necessity entail understanding the referring agent, the client's environment, and the broader context in which interventions are to be made. These issues are discussed in Chapter 6.

3

WRITTEN ENGLISH AND THE GIVEN-NEW CONTRACT

Analysis of typical difficulties with report writing – from the perspective of readers and writers – shows that a central difficulty in writing reports is often the writer's failure to understand the complex and subtle relation of spoken to written language. In this chapter, a framework is presented for understanding discourse comprehension through the psycholinguistic concepts discussed by Clark (Clark, 1985; Clark & Clark, 1977, pp. 91-93; Clark & Haviland, 1977). The framework then is applied to report writing in order to show how writers can produce sentences and paragraphs that will be understood by readers of their reports. Other report writing problems are discussed in later chapters, and this chapter's psycholinguistic framework is expanded into a model that provides solutions to them. Before we discuss the problems specific to report writing, it will be useful to detail how certain psycholinguistic concepts about discourse comprehension (understanding presentations of topical material) can be applied to written English. Examples are provided later in the chapter so that you can practice applying the model to reporting test data, but the discussion begins with an explanation of how written English differs from spoken English.

Written and Spoken English

Written English bears a deceptively simple relation to the spoken language. The vocabulary and syntax of written English (the way words are organized into sentences) may seem familiar, but when you write down what you might say to someone else, it usually won't read sensibly and may be misleading or impossible to understand. Why is this so? Imagine the following situation. A young psychologist arrives at a group office on Monday morning looking forward (at least) to having a cup of coffee and a doughnut. She expects them to be there, based on her past experience that someone at the office will have made coffee by the time she arrives and that another person will have purchased doughnuts. When she actually arrives, however, she sees a colleague taking the last doughnut from the box. The secretary, sympathetic to the psychologist's plight, responds to her questioning look with "He took the last one." In this situation, it is immediately clear to the psychologist what the secretary means. "He" refers to the colleague, "took" to the activity of removing the doughnut from the box, and "last one" to the only remaining doughnut.

Now imagine that the psychologist arrives at her office on the same morning, but before going to look for coffee and doughnuts, she finds a note on her desk. The thoughtful secretary has left a message: "He took the last one." It should be immediately apparent that the psychologist will have to ask the secretary for clarification of the message.

This example illustrates that speakers can rely on many sources of information in addition to the words used in oral communication. As we speak, we consciously and unconsciously take in listeners' facial expressions and postures. In addition, we share context, as in the example above in which the context of the communication determined to a great extent the meaning of the message. When communication is in written form, as in psychological reports, these aids are not present; much more of the communicative burden falls on the meanings of the words and their organization. The writer must assess carefully the extent to which the reader will comprehend the context of the communication. For example, discussion of psychological test data in a report takes place in a context that is quite different when the discussants are both psychologists than when one is a lay person. These facts require the writer to develop expertise in using these more restricted tools for communicating the complex ideas contained in psychological reports.

The Given-new Contract

Clark (Clark, 1985; Clark & Clark, 1977; Clark & Haviland, 1977) suggests that during a conversation an implicit contract exists between speaker and listener. This is part of the general process termed *coordination*, by which speakers and listeners cooperate in the communication process so that they are mutually intelligible (Clark, 1985). Clark calls it the *given-new contract*, a name that emphasizes the essential requirement that two persons engaging in effective communication must agree on a basic idea (the *given*) before something can be said about it (the *new*). Clark and Clark (1977) explain:

> The speaker agrees (a) to use given information to refer to information she thinks the listener can uniquely identify from what he already knows and (b) to use new information to refer to information she believes to be true but is not already known to the listener (p. 92).

In the example above, when the secretary used the word "He" in a context in which it clearly referred to the colleague taking the donut; "He" was the given element in the sentence. The new element was "took the last one."

A similar contract can be postulated to exist between reader and writer. Evidence on comprehension of reading shows that prior knowledge influences how much a reader understands, a finding that supports the extension of the given-new contract concept to written prose (e.g., Entin & Klare, 1985). In order for the reader to feel that the writer has communicated effectively (indeed, to understand the writer at all), this contract cannot be violated. What circumstances, then, can result in a violation, and how can they be avoided?

An answer to these questions may be found by examining the meaning of the given-new contract in the context of the psychological report. It can be violated at three points in the sequence: (1) the *given* may not, in fact, be shared information; (2) the link between *given* and *new* may not be logical; and (3) the new information is not explained clearly or is not unique new information about the given. At each step in the communication process defined by the contract, then, the process can be subverted.

The first step requires that the writer be reasonably certain that the given element is a *shared referent*. Shared referents are whatever the psychologist can reasonably assume that he or she has in common with the reader. A concrete description of the client's behavior, such as "His voice trembled and was quite low as he spoke," provides an image with which the reader is probably familiar, and the psychologist can assume it constitutes a shared referent. On the other hand, a statement such as "The primed 2-7 profile code suggests the presence of considerable anxiety and depression" may be meaningless to readers not trained in MMPI interpretation, to whom the phrase "primed 2-7 code" will be jargon. Thus, one way in which the given-new contract can be violated in psychological reports is by using terms as givens when they are not shared referents with the reader. The use of jargon or technical terms whose meanings are unknown to the reader is one of the most common violations of this sort. Without a common base for understanding, the reader is at a loss at the outset in trying to understand the writer.

The second way in which the given-new contract can also be violated arises when the new element is not related clearly to the given. The logical transition from given to new cannot be too abrupt or, most importantly, cannot be contrary to the reader's expectations without clear justification. To use the example above, even though the image of a person's voice trembling and being low is a shared referent, if the next statement is "showing that he was quite happy" the reader predictably will balk. In this instance, the flow of logic from the given to the new is interrupted. If the writer supplies additional information, such as that the low and trembling voice is characteristic of this client when experiencing strong emotion, the flow will not be interrupted and the contract will not be violated.

The third way in which the contract can be violated is when the new information isn't explained clearly or isn't unique. This type of violation can arise in several contexts. When the new information is actually old information, little harm is done. When the new information contradicts expectations or is inconsistent with other information, however, it may be critical to provide additional explanations. If it was customary for the staff to purchase two boxes of donuts and only one is present and it is empty, the helpful secretary discussed above might be required to explain, "We only got one box today." The additional information might sufficiently clarify the situation for the unfortunate psychologist.

A special instance of the third type of violation occurs when the new is made to appear informative, but is in fact so vague or general that little or no new information is imparted. An example of this type of statement is, "She is a person who is concerned about her feelings." This statement is both quite vague and true of nearly everyone. This category of given-new contract violation is referred to variously as the "Barnum effect" or as an "Aunt Fanny" statements (Klopfer, 1960; Tallent, 1976). Barnum statements often are defined as overly general statements, while Aunt Fanny statements are defined by the fact that they are universally true, so that one can say it is also true about "my Aunt Fanny."

Understanding the three major categories of violations of the given-new contract helps make sense out of much of the research on reader satisfaction with psychological reports. This topic is considered further in Chapter 4. First, however, it is necessary to review other basic ideas about written English.

How to Write Intelligibly

Consideration of written English from the point of view of the given-new contract leads to a general formula for writing intelligibly.

1. *Be sure that the given element in the sentence is a shared referent.* This requires that you carefully consider the person for whom you are writing the report. In writing a report for another psychologist, reporting Wechsler scale or MMPI scores and drawing inferences directly from them may be appropriate. On the other hand, in writing for someone not familiar with psychological testing, it may be necessary to provide more explanation. Statements such as "Andrea's performance on a subtest which required that she quickly assemble puzzles of common objects. . . ," or "Persons who obtain this score are often seen by others as feeling sad, 'blue,' or depressed" convey images that are probably shared experiences with your reader. A writer can be fairly certain that most readers know what puzzles are and what the activity of assembling them involves and, similarly, that most persons know how a person who feels "blue" behaves.

2. *Be sure that the relation between the given (shared referent) and the new is clear.* An abrupt or illogical transition from the given to the new element will confuse the reader. The flow from the shared referent or given to the new data provided by the report must be unmistakably clear. If the new information is unexpected or appears contradictory to other information, additional explanations may be required.

3. *Be sure that the information that is presented as new is in fact both new and sufficiently meaningful.* Repeated presentations of statements that are broadly or generally true can create a report that gives a false sense of having communicated important information about a client without having done so. In addition to being an extremely poor assessment practice, it is not in the client's best interest for you to make vague statements. It is likely, for example, that recommendations based on such statements will be ill founded and unpersuasive to readers.

Repeated violations of the implicit agreement between writer and reader to honor the given-new contract will annoy or confuse the reader and should be avoided. In what follows it is assumed that if you stop to think, you can make a good guess about the referents you share with your readers. It is also possible to assess systematically readers' knowledge of terms that might be used (Ownby & Wallbrown, 1983). When not sure, it is a good idea to provide additional explanation. Logical transitions between givens and new elements, however, are a more complex issue and are discussed further in the next section.

Sentences

You may recall from classes in elementary school that a sentence can be defined as "a group of words that expresses a complete thought." What the teacher didn't explain, however, was how to tell whether a complete thought had been expressed. Usually, you were left to "feel" whether it was true. An alternative definition of a sentence among grammarians has been that it consists of a subject and predicate. Presumably, if both are present, a complete, although potentially illogical, thought is expressed. This definition is easier to make operational.

Imagine reading the following sentence outside the context of a report:

The child   /   gazed out the window.

Thinking back to your lessons in prescriptive grammar, you may recall that the phrase "The child" is the subject and "gazed out the window" is the predicate. The sentence works as a grammatical example, but chances are you don't feel that you've been told anything important about a particular child.

Take, for example, the case of Joey Brown, an 11-year-old in Ms. Taylor's fifth-grade class, referred for not paying attention in class and not completing class work. Note how much more vivid the following sentence is:

Joey Brown   /   gazed out the window.

Why is it more vivid? You might answer correctly that it is more specific, but a more compelling reason for its vividness is that "the child" was at best a vaguely shared referent: my idea of "the child" and yours are probably different. On the other hand, both of our concepts of "Joey Brown" include a number of elements, such as the facts that he's 11, a boy, in Ms. Taylor's class, and referred for evaluation because of inattention. In other words, Joey is a shared referent.

To generalize from this example, it can be seen that the subject of a sentence corresponds to the given of the given-new contract. The new, then, is the part of the sentence that provides additional information about the given, or the predicate. If you were a reader of the sentence about Joey, you probably knew something about him at the outset, but until you were told, you didn't know the possibly important fact that he gazed out the window during class.

Most declarative sentences in psychological reports are more complex than this example, but follow the same basic structure. This leads to the following formula: *to write an intelligible sentence in a report, you say something new about a shared referent.* Consider this example, which might appear in a report about Joey Brown:

Joey achieved an IQ score of 118.

Here, the given, "Joey," has been established previously in the report by placing his first and last names at the top of the report, probably along with other identifying information. The psychologist also may have explained why finding out Joey's IQ was worth the trouble of administering the test in the "Reason for Referral" section of the report. The new (something the reader didn't know, but was interested in finding out) is that his IQ is 118. The writer of this sentence has started with something shared with the reader—knowledge of Joey—and told the reader something new about him. Notice how this seemingly simple example follows the prescribed elements of the contract. The given is truly a shared referent, the link is logical because it is quite reasonable that a child should obtain an IQ score when administered an IQ test, and the new information is specific and unique.

Here is an example for practicing the skill of linking sentence elements. The shared referent continues to be Joey; additional information is provided for you to create a declarative statement that consists of a given and a new.

GIVEN: Joey Brown
NEW: Standard score on a reading achievement test = 85

One construction from these two elements might be: "Joey achieved a standard score on a reading achievement test of 85."

Here is another example for practice:

GIVEN: Joey Brown
NEW: Poor performance on geometric drawing task.

A construction from these elements might be: "Joey's performance on a geometric drawing task was poor." Additional examples for you to practice on are provided in Appendix A.

Although it might be possible to write a report that consists only of these simple declarative sentences, each containing just one given and one new element, the writing that would result would seem dull or monotonous. Rather than simply putting two declarative sentences on paper, most writers prefer to vary sentence length so that what is written is more interesting to the reader. For example, you might want to vary sentence length by adding a second related fact to the first in reporting Joey's IQ:

GIVEN: Joey Brown
NEW: He achieved an IQ score of 118.
NEW: An IQ score of 118 is in the high average range of general intellectual ability.

Various grammatic constructions can be used to make writing less monotonous. Although there are more precise terms for such constructions, they can be thought of, in general, as expressing some type of relation between two or more ideas. A common way of combining two ideas is the *absolute construction* that allows *coordination* between them:

> Joey achieved an IQ score of 118, showing that he is probably functioning in the high average range of general intellectual ability.

In this construction, two ideas have been linked by the word "showing." Also note that a second given-new sequence is present. This time, the given,"he," refers to Joey and the new is the statement about high average intellectual function. This type of construction indicates the equivalence of the two elements. Other relations are indicated by other constructions, such as *contrast* (for example, "She did well on Test A *but* poorly on Test B) or *elaboration* ("She did well on Test A *and* Test B").

Try using contrast with the following given-new elements:

GIVEN: Joey Brown
NEW: High average intellectual function
NEW: Low average reading achievement

One way of relating these two contradictory new elements would be to contrast them by writing "Joey scored in the high average range of general intellectual ability, but in the low average range in reading achievement."

Try using elaboration with these elements:

GIVEN: Joey Brown
NEW: Poor performance on geometric drawings
NEW: Illegible handwriting

Here again, a simple way of relating these elements through elaboration would be to write, "Joey performed poorly on a geometric drawing task, and his handwriting was illegible."

Mastering the process of writing declarative sentences is central to expository writing, which is what psychological reports are all about. Three important relations between givens and news have been demonstrated: (a) equivalence via the absolute construction; (b) contrast; (c) elaboration.

Paragraphs

Just as a report cannot consist of a series of short declarative sentences alone, nor can it be made up of just one long sentence. Written English is organized into groups of related sentences called *paragraphs*. Paragraphs allow for information to be sorted into higher-level units of meaning that contain a series of logically related sentences. You may recall from your previous instruction in writing that a paragraph often contains a *topic sentence* and a number of other sentences. If we return to the framework provided by the given-new contract in considering paragraphs, the topic sentence can be defined as a given-new statement in which the new is phrased generally and requires substantiation. This definition can be clarified with an example.

Suppose that you are engaged in a political discussion with a friend about the relative merits of candidate Bombast. You might begin by saying "Bombast is the best person for the office," but, noticing the dubious look in your friend's eye, you decide to furnish substantiating details. You might say something such as "Bombast is for mom, apple pie, and progressive social legislation," and perhaps even attempt to clinch your argument by citing "Bombast is for pay raises for psychologists." In this case, you've begun with a given-new statement in which the new is phrased generally ("Bombast is the best person for the office") and continued with substantiating details (Bombast's positions on the issues).

This point can be illustrated further by the results of Joey's assessment. Suppose that several measures of general intellectual ability have been administered because determination of Joey's intellectual abilities is an important issue for those who are working with him—perhaps there is a question about lateralized brain dysfunction, his ability to profit from verbal psychotherapy, or his eligibility for special education services in the schools. You plan a paragraph in your report on Joey's intellectual ability as estimated by the Wechsler Intelligence Scale for Children—Revised (WISC-R), the Peabody Picture Vocabulary Test—Revised (PPVT-R, measuring receptive vocabulary), and the Raven's Progressive Matrices (Raven's, measuring nonverbal reasoning abilities).

To utilize the psycholinguistic framework for paragraph construction, you would begin with a statement about Joey's abilities which includes a given and a generally phrased new that requires substantiation: "Joey's test scores show that he is probably functioning in the high average range of general intellectual ability." The given is "Joey," and the generally phrased new is the description of his overall level of intellectual functioning. This statement now can be substantiated by a series of given-new sequences that detail test results. Note that in these sequences the given becomes the tests administered (with which the reader is already familiar), and the new elements will be the test results. The final product might be:

> Joey's test scores show that he is probably functioning in the high-average range of general intellectual ability. His scores on the WISC-R suggest this because his Verbal IQ was 116, his Performance IQ was 120, and his Full Scale IQ was 118. His scores on the PPVT-R and the Raven's tend to confirm these estimates, as they were at standard scores of 114 and 119, respectively. It is thus unlikely that low intellectual abilities account for his academic difficulties in school.

The last sentence, beginning "It is thus likely. . . ," illustrates one other component of a well-constructed paragraph. This is a summary sentence which draws a conclusion, relates the paragraph's meaning to the referral, provides a link to the next paragraph, or accomplishes a combination of these functions.

Although writing a paragraph within these guidelines at first may seem awkward, it can become natural with practice. Two examples follow. Each brief sentence contains test data related to a particular point. The task is to write a generally phrased given-new sequence as the first sentence of each paragraph, put the data into proper relation (using elaboration, coordination, or contrast), and write a summary sentence to conclude each of your paragraphs.

Example I. Paul is a 32-year-old man referred for evaluation of apparent depression:

1. Paul's scores on the Minnesota Multiphasic Personality Inventory (MMPI) were significantly high on scales 2 (Depression) and 7 (agitated anxiety).

2. Paul's responses to questions were brief and tended to express despair and hopelessness.

3. Paul's score on the Beck Depression Inventory (BDI) was 35, usually interpreted as representing "severe" depression.

4. Paul's movements were slow.

Here is one way to combine these ideas into a paragraph:

Results of this assessment indicate that Paul is severely depressed. Results of the MMPI, for example, show that he is probably experiencing feelings of sadness and despair. The results of the BDI also indicate that he is depressed because Paul's score on this measure usually is interpreted as reflecting severe depression. Observation of Paul during testing confirms this impression. His movements were slow and his responses to questions brief and full of despair and hoplessness. Overall, it appears quite clear that Paul is severely depressed.

Example II. Michelle is a 14-year-old girl referred for evaluation of acting-out behavior at school and at home:

1. Michelle's scores on the Personality Inventory for Children (PIC) were significantly elevated on the DEP (Depression) scale.

2. Michelle's behavior during testing alternated between defiant uncooperativeness and crying.

3. The referring source, a local family psychiatrist, reports that Michelle's parents were recently divorced and that Michelle continues to live with her mother.

4. Michelle's teacher reports that, until recently, she has been an exemplary student and that she has never been a behavior problem before.

5. An interview with Michelle's mother suggests that Michelle may blame her mother for her parents' divorce.

Here is one way this information can be organized into a paragraph:

Results of this assessment show that Michelle's acting-out behavior may stem from her anger about her parents' divorce, to which she has reacted by becoming depressed. Several data sources support this idea—Michelle's score on the DEP scale of the PIC was significantly elevated, which suggests that she is experiencing feelings of sadness. Her behavior during testing ranged from defiant uncooperativeness to crying, again suggesting both depression and anger. Finally, an interview with Michelle's mother suggests that Michelle may blame her mother for her parents' divorce and that her acting-out behavior could be an attempt to gain revenge against her. Therefore, it is unlikely that Michelle's behavior represents a long-standing pattern of maladaptive behavior, but, rather, is a reaction to a current life event.

Organization of Paragraphs in the Report

Ultimately, the paragraphs constructed in this way must be combined into the coherent entity of the full report. Most report writers organize paragraphs into the larger sections of the report outline. The sections of the report outline tend to give the report a logical flow from referral question to recommendations. Writers usually include sections such as "Reason for Referral," "Background Information," "Assessment Results," and "Summary and Recommendations." This organizational scheme gives the report a sequential flow that follows the steps in the evaluation process so that the reader of the report can recreate in his or her own mind the process by which the psychologist reaches the conclusions stated in the report. Paragraphs within these sections follow a similar sequential format and list data in logical order. The precise way in which data is presented, however, depends on the report format. These issues are discussed in detail in Chapter 6.

In the next chapter, specific problems in report writing are considered, and solutions to these problems are presented in the form of an expanded psycholinguistic model for report writing.

4

THE EXPOSITORY PROCESS MODEL

As suggested in the last chapter, the given-new contract can be helpful in learning how to write better sentences and paragraphs. This approach provides important conceptual tools for understanding the ways in which writers communicate meanings to the reader. In this chapter, the problems made evident by a survey of research on reports are reviewed from this perspective as an introduction to the expository process model (EPM). This model applies the psycholinguistic approach directly to the problems of report writing and allows a fairly specific prescription of how to write reports.

Language Usage Problems

Language usage problems stem from several types of violations of the given-new contract, at the levels of the given, the relation of the given to the new, and the new itself. One important usage problem indicated in the literature is that reports often contain terms whose meanings are unclear to report recipients. It may be helpful to investigate routinely whether your readers in fact understand the terms you use: once, at a party, a psychologist friend related how he used Ownby and Wallbrown's (1983) suggestions for obtaining feedback about reports and discovered to his surprise that a teacher with many years of experience didn't understand the term "visual-motor skills." The moral here is not to assume that readers will understand even terms that you think are quite basic.

In the case cited above, the writer mistakenly had assumed that the term was a shared referent and, therefore, could be used as a given, when it actually required further explanation. In this instance, the term "visual-motor skills" should have been referenced to a concrete description, as suggested by a number of studies reviewed in Chapter 1. The psychologist might have said, for example, "Veronica's visual-motor skills were assessed as her ability to copy geometric designs with pencil and paper." In this way, the term "visual-motor skills" is referenced to a concrete explanation, which makes the term a shared referent rather than jargon.

A similar, but more difficult problem is the use of test scores in reports. Psychologists often assume that a score as commonly used as the intelligence quotient (IQ) means the same thing to everyone. A brief discussion of such basic statistical concepts as standard error of measurement or confidence intervals with a group of nonpsychologists probably will show disagreements among lay persons and even among the psychologists. This is what Rucker (1967b) found in the study reviewed in Chapter 1. It is more difficult to give concrete explanations of the meaning of test scores, but with some ingenuity it is possible. Wechsler subtests, for example, can be described as "explaining the meanings of words," (Vocabulary) or "putting together puzzles of common objects" (Object Assembly). Other examples of how to describe subtests are provided in Appendix C. Further, although most persons are unfamiliar with the precise meaning of Wechsler scaled scores, a client's score on a subtest can be converted easily to standard or percentile rank score, which are interpreted much more easily.

Research on reporting showed that readers often feel that raw assessment data should be included in the report. It should be recognized that linking report data (such as behavioral observations and test scores) to conclusions and recommendations in a meaningful way often requires the use of terms such as "visual-motor skills" and "depression." Such constructs, however, may be little more than empty jargon to the reader if they are neither already shared referents nor made into shared referents by linking them with lower-level shared referents such as behavioral descriptions, as illustrated above with Veronica's visual-motor skills. Any failure to estimate whether such terms are truly shared referents will be yet another violation of the given-new contract.

Content Problems

As noted, most content problems with reports often are related to disagreements between the writer and the report's recipients about the purpose of the report. Studies have shown, for example, that psychiatrists may view specific therapeutic recommendations as inappropriate content for reports, while teachers in public schools may criticize reports for failing to provide extensive recommendations about how to teach the child assessed. Thus, report recipients vary widely in their willingness to accept direction from psychologists. This contrast once again highlights the need for the psychologist to assess the context into which the report will go, including the needs and interests of the referral source. This topic is discussed extensively in Chapter 5.

A similar failure to assess the reader might lead psychologists to neglect the need to present a balanced picture of the client. Studies that show that certain types of information in reports can influence attitudes toward clients, including the extent to which the report's reader believes that he or she can intervene effectively with the client, indicate that the psychologist should describe not only weaknesses, but also strengths of the client. Assuming that the reader wants suggestions about how to work with the client, it is likely that he or she will feel more competent in dealing with a client if the report includes a discussion of specific strategies for intervening with the client's problem. In this case, there will be no violation of the given-new contract if the report provides a full and balanced description of the client and detailed recommendations about how to help him or her.

Organizational Problems

Few studies have addressed organizational problems in reports, perhaps because they are minor in comparison to other difficulties. It's worth noting, for example, that studies by Pryzwansky and Hanania (1986) and Wiener (1985, 1987; Wiener & Kohler, 1986) showed that the traditional report format is preferred by many consumers in educational settings. Results of this study are also consistent with what we find when the given-new distinction is applied at this level of organization. The dictates of the contract allow us to determine what sort of organization the most effective report is likely to have.

It is assumed that the given element is the client—what the assessor and the report's recipients have in common. The new element is the assessment information. Therefore, the report's organizational format should establish clearly the given, provide relevant information about the assessment's context and purpose, explain assessment results in a way that the reader will understand, and provide succinct conclusions coupled with a suggested course of action. Finally, the information contained in these sections must flow logically toward the summary and recommendations.

Purpose of the Report

Here, the given-new contract is related only indirectly to the question of how to write the report. Given that the purpose of the report is to provide credible and persuasive statements about clients, it can be said that consistently honoring the given-new contract can affect dramatically the extent to which a report's purpose is achieved. It is possible to go so far as to say that statements that are not readily understood are unlikely to be either credible or persuasive, which would make it unlikely that the report would produce the desired attitude or behavior change.

The Expository Process Model

Viewed overall, the research findings and recommendations of authorities seem contradictory. Jargon is to be avoided, but, as noted, terms such as "visual-motor skills" or "depression" often must be used to explain basic assessment data. Thus, the writer is left with the problem of reporting the assessment in a way that includes data, but that excludes common terms for explaining the meaning of the data. The writer somehow must navigate a dangerous strait between merely reporting test scores and using jargon to explain what they mean.

While some might regard this as merely a problem of writing well, closer scrutiny of the problem suggests that the answer is not so simple. The issue of jargon in reports is usually not only a question of using particular terms, but also a question of the fundamental process of relating the basic data to conclusions drawn from them. Psychologists usually accomplish this by integrating assessment data within an implicit or explicit theory of abilities or personality and then explaining the data in terms of this theory. A psychologist, for example, who believes that the structure of human intellectual abilities can best be understood as one central ability, *g*, might not emphasize differences between Verbal and Performance IQs on the Wechsler scales in reporting results of intelligence tests. By contrast, the neuropsychologist may view such differences as indications of relative impairment of one of the cerebral hemispheres. In this case, he or she probably will stress the presence of a Verbal-Performance discrepancy in the report.

The problem with the way in which psychologists report assessments is not in their use of professional terms (often called jargon), but, rather, a failure of writers to make explicit the relation of the underlying theory (in psychological terms) to the data upon which the report is based. It is this problem that the expository process model addresses. By clarifying the relation between the assessment data and the psychologist's interpretation of them, the model helps psychologists to use their theories more effectively in reporting. The model requires that the writer make the relation between assessment data and terms used in his or her theory explicit and that both of these elements be related logically to the recommendations and conclusions contained within the report. A key term used in the model is "middle-level construct," first introduced by Appelbaum (1970). The next section explains in detail what middle-level constructs are, as a preliminary to presenting the model itself.

Middle-level Constructs

Appelbaum, in a classic article, discusses how the writer relates assessment data to conclusions when reporting an evaluation:

> When making inferences, the tester observes individual behaviors, moves to higher levels of abstraction as he connects observations, and moves down again to more data in order to check and extend his inferences — all these steps being guided by his theory (1970, p. 352).

In this context, "theory" refers not only to whether the psychologist is psychodynamically or behaviorally oriented, but also to the less abstract concepts that he or she invokes in order to explain the client's behavior. While these constructs often are related to higher-level theoretical allegiances, they may be related equally often to the elemental constructs with which the psychologist thinks about the client's ability structure or emotional functioning. Appelbaum calls these terms "middle-level constructs," lying as they do between the lowest level of raw assessment data and the highest abstraction of formal theory.

Middle-level constructs are probably the very jargon for which reports are criticized. Examples of middle-level constructs are such terms as "intelligence," "perceptual skills," "anxiety," or "neurosis." They are terms that are commonly used in explanations of clients' behavior, but that often do not have a precise shared definition. You can imagine, for example, asking 100 psychologists to define the term "intelligence." It's likely that they would give you 100 definitions (at least!). Middle-level constructs are useful because they give psychologists a set of terms for communicating with each other. Without the term "intelligence," it might be difficult or awkward to discuss individual differences in problem-solving skills, even though psychologists often disagree about what "intelligence" really is. Because they mean different things to different persons, middle-level constructs easily can become jargon, or meaningless terms, when they are used in psychological reports without due care to prevent violations of the given-new contract.

You also can see that these constructs can be useful in moving back and forth through the more abstract steps between data and conclusions described by Appelbaum because they provide the reader with conceptual bridges between each part of the writer's logic. We are then confronted, however, with the research findings already discussed above, which show that using these terms does not always help the reader to understand, but may, in fact, hinder him or her. How can this paradox be resolved?

One answer lies in the way in which middle-level constructs are used by writers. A number of authors, for example, have commented on the need to provide data, such as observations and test responses, within the report as a way of helping the reader understand the author's conclusions. To cite Appelbaum once again: "By thus offering the reader a sense of underlying data founded on normative experience, the psychologist makes his theoretical remarks less abstruse" (p. 352). Given the need for data within the report and the potential usefulness of middle-level constructs, the possibility emerges that what is wrong with the use of these constructs in reports is not their content—the terms themselves—but their relation to what the reader already knows (the degree to which they are shared referents) or their relation to the client (the degree to which the middle-level constructs are clearly related to the purpose of the assessment). In terms of the given-new contract, any of the three types of violations can occur. The construct can be used as a given when it is not truly a shared referent, the relation between the given information and a new construct can be unclear, or the construct can be used as a new when its meaning is not at all clear.

Researchers often have demonstrated that reading comprehension is related to prior knowledge of subject matter. (See Entin & Klare, 1985.) If this research can be applied to reporting, it suggests that readers will understand the writer's statements best when they have a background knowledge of what the report is about. Briefly stated, if a middle-level construct is not related clearly to data in the report or to what the reader already knows, it will appear groundless or not be understood. If the middle-level construct has no clear relation to the purpose of the report in providing conclusions and recommendations about the client, it will seem irrelevant and distracting.

The hypothesis that what's wrong with middle-level constructs is not the terms themselves, but how they are used in reports leads to a model for writing sentences and paragraphs in reports. The expository process model proposes the following about how to use middle-level constructs:

I. *Any middle-level construct used in a report must have a directly shared referent in data either implicitly or explicitly contained in the report.*

This statement means that all middle-level constructs used in a report must be clearly related to something both the reader and writer know about. For example, before the writer can make the statement "auditory perceptual skills are poor," he or she must have determined that "auditory perceptual skills" is a phrase that is a shared referent with the report's intended recipient, as might be the case when a psychologist writes a report to a speech pathologist.

If the phrase is not a shared referent, it should be made into one by referencing it to a concrete description. It might be possible to state, for example, that "The client's auditory perceptual skills were assessed as his ability to break words down into their component sounds." In this case, the subsequent statement that these skills are poor has a clear meaning for the reader.

II. *Conclusions are evaluative statements about the middle-level construct and must also be supported by data.*

Conclusions are evaluative statements that say something about the degree or extent of the construct. These evaluative statements also must be supported by data in the report. For example, the statement "the client's level of anxiety is significantly high" includes the middle-level construct "anxiety" and the conclusion "is significantly high." Such a statement, according to the model, must be supported by reference to data. In this case, the reference might be that the client's score on scale 7 of the MMPI was 85, which will produce the following: "The client's level of anxiety is significantly high — her score on scale 7 of the MMPI was a T of 85."

III. *Recommendations must be logically related to conclusions stated in the report.*

This proposal specifies that the recommendations be clearly derived from the construct and the conclusion. Although a recommendation for a psychiatric evaluation might be appropriate for a client, it should not be made in a report if the reason for it has not been established previously. The groundwork for each recommendation, therefore, must be laid in the preceding sections of the report.

The three proposals of the model are derived directly from the observation, made explicit in research studies, that the reader of the report wants a well-reasoned explanation of how the psychologist arrived at his or her conclusions. Figure 2 graphically represents the model and shows the progressive steps of moving from data to higher levels of abstraction from those data to recommendations.

It should be noted that these steps do not have to be immediately contiguous within the report. Data can be presented in one section, middle-level constructs in another, conclusions presented in yet another, and recommendations appended as a list at the end

FIGURE 2

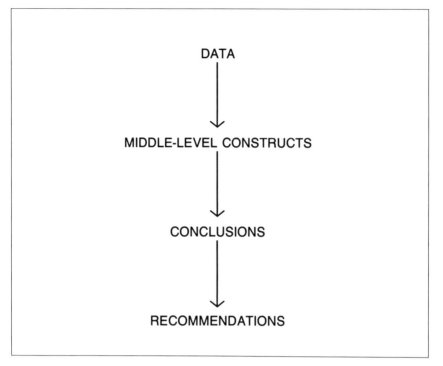

of the report. What is critical is that the constituents logically follow each other and that their relation is apparent to the reader. In some cases, it may be best to place raw data and constructs together because the construct is usually a significant abstraction from the data, and clarity may require that this relation be understood easily.

Examples may help to illustrate how the model can be applied and the benefits that can result from developing better sentences. Here is an example of a non-model statement that begins with a middle-level construct:

> Visual-motor skills are poor, and work on remedial tasks such as puzzles and tracing is recommended.

Parsing this example according to the model, a middle-level construct ("visual-motor skills") is presented with a conclusion (they are "poor") and a recommendation ("use puzzles and tracing"). The absence of elaboration of the middle-level construct prevents elaboration of the conclusion and recommendation because without supporting data, a highly specific recommendation such as "use puzzles" is not obviously needed. Although the recommendation follows logically, it is not immediately clear to the reader in what way working with puzzles or tracing may help in developing "visual-motor skills."

Contrast the first example with the following model-based one:

> The client had difficulty with several tasks, such as copying drawings and putting together puzzles of common objects. These difficulties suggest the client has poor visual-motor skills and that work on tracing tasks and putting together puzzles may help her develop these skills.

Parsing this example, it can be seen that its elements include, in sequence, data ("copying drawings" and "putting together puzzles"), a middle-level construct ("visual-motor skills"), a conclusion (they are "poor") and the same recommendation as in the first example (use "tracing tasks and puzzles").

Here is another example of a non-model statement:

> The client appears depressed, and it is recommended that he be seen by a psychotherapist.

Here is the model-based equivalent:

> The client's behavior during assessment, which included frequent sighs, rare smiles, and crying, suggests that he is depressed. It is recommended that he be seen by a psychotherapist.

Once again, the model-based statement may be seen to be more vivid and to communicate the psychologist's message in a more concrete and easily understandable fashion.

Several studies of this model (Ownby, 1984, 1990a, 1990b) have shown that various groups of report consumers (a group of parents and educational specialists in Ownby, 1984) and persons familiar with reporting (clinical and counseling psychologists in Ownby, 1990a; school psychologists in Ownby, 1990b) rated model-based statements as significantly more credible and persuasive than similar non-model-based statements. Additional data analysis, not reported in the papers, suggested that the effect that caused higher ratings of model-based statements could be separated into effects due to sentence length and due to the characteristics of the model-based sentence. The effect due to the model continued to be significant when the effect due to sentence length was controlled statistically. Thus, it appears that the logical relations between data, middle-level constructs, conclusions, and recommendations are clarified by the structure imposed by the model and that this clarification makes a difference in how readers rate statements.

Advantages of using the model for report writing are that it provides a clear structure for writing effective statements and that it can be used by psychologists independent of their theoretical orientation. Expository process model-based statements are, by definition, data-based and logical because the structure of the model ensures that the logical argument in the statement proceeds step-by-step from data to conclusions. There is nothing magical about the model, of course, but it does provide a specific formula for implementing the recommendations of a number of experts on how to use data and technical terms in reports.

The Model with Paragraphs

At a more complex level, the model can be used to build statements at progressively higher levels of abstraction from data, whether one is building from several bits of data or from several already supported middle-level constructs. The schematic for this more complex organization is suggested in Figure 3.

This diagram presents the possible macrostructure of model-based reports. Various types and quantities of data, depending on their distinctiveness (as in the case of behavioral observations) or validity and departure from the norm (as in the case of test scores) may be used to infer middle-level constructs. One data element may lead to one construct and one resulting conclusion and recommendation (Fig. 3, line 1). Lines 2 to 4 of Figure 3 present progressively more complex instances of the possible relations of data to middle-level constructs, conclusions, and recommendations. It can be seen, for example, that several bits of data may contribute to the different constructs, one construct can contribute to several conclusions, and that other, even more complex combinations are possible.

FIGURE 3

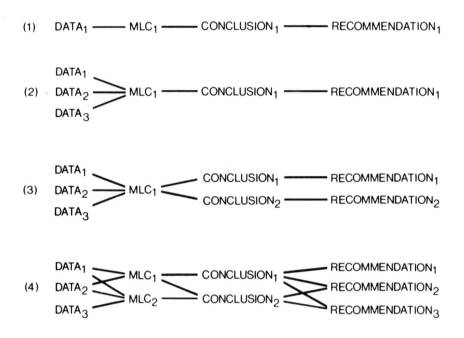

Construct-conclusion sequences also can stand alone when their implications for the client's situation are obvious (for example, when the sequence were "abilities are normal"), or they may lead to higher-order conclusions, which can include an evaluative constituent and other explanations that make the conclusions more understandable to the reader.

Again, examples can serve to clarify these points. Here is part of a set of data obtained during the evaluation of a school-age child:

1. John made impulsive errors in sight word recognition;
2. John's scaled score on the Digit Span subtest of the WISC-R was 6; Coding was 4; Arithmetic was 6;
3. John's classroom teacher reports that he is more impulsive and active than his classmates;
4. John's principal reports that he is defiant of authority;
5. John's teachers report that he often does not respond to their requests;

6. John's scores on a behavior rating scale indicate that he displays an unusual amount of acting-out behavior.

Data from statements 1 to 3 could be used to infer the middle-level constructs of "attentional skills deficits," which, in turn, could lead to a conclusion of the presence of "attention deficit-hyperactivity disorder." Such a conclusion could lead to recommendations for cognitive behavior modification interventions, medical evaluation for the possible use of stimulant medication, and perhaps special tutoring in reading skills. Data from statements 4 to 6 might lead to the inference "problems in impulse control," which by itself could lead to recomendations for behavioral treatment. Note also that a conclusion, as intended in the model, can consist only of an evaluative statement about the nature of a middle-level construct, as with "problems in impulse control." In this case, the logical flow to recommendations is understandable to the reader without further discussion.

Depending on the severity of the problem, however, and on other factors, some psychologists might go further and infer the presence of "conduct disorder," a conclusion that might lead to recommendations about classroom management, family counseling, or special class placement. Note also in these examples, in contrast to those already presented, that while the conclusion is still evaluative it can include the inference of a disorder's presence.

Recalling the definition of a paragraph from Chapter 2, it is now possible to apply the model in the writing paragraphs. That definition stated that paragraphs consist of three elements:

1. a topic sentence that includes a given-new sequence in which the new is phrased generally and requires substantiation;
2. several given-new sequences that provide substantiation of the new in the topic sentence;
3. a final statement that summarizes the paragraph, relates its meaning to the referral question, provides flow to the next paragraph, or some combination of these.

In terms of the model, the generally phrased new element in the topic sentence could be a middle-level construct whose relevance to the client's functioning is clarified through assessment data. We will call paragraphs with this sort of structure "type I." An example follows:

> This assessment suggests that Sybil is depressed. She often sighed and occasionally cried during test administration. When asked, she acknowledged feeling a negative mood and said she often feels "What's the use?" Her scores on the MMPI reflect this as well. Her T score of 82 on scale 2 is often interpreted as reflecting a significant feeling of negativism and low mood. Taken together, these results indicate the presence of functionally significant depression, which is at least a partial explanation for her recent poor work and school performance.

The phrase "Sybil is depressed" is element one, the topic sentence, and elements such as "T score of 82" are the second element, given-new sequences that substantiate the topic sentence. The last sentence is the third element, the final summary statement.
Here is another example:

> These results show that John is probably suffering from a significant anxiety disorder. His own description of his concerns, which include feelings of panic and terror, is consistent with this idea. Observations of him during an episode of severe anxiety are also consistent—he was clearly agitated, was trembling, and was difficult to communicate with at the time. These results show that his concerns probably arise from an anxiety disorder rather than a heart condiditon, especially because his physician reports that the latter condition is not present.

It may be helpful to you to try and determine which elements in this paragraph correspond to the three elements of the type I paragraph.

An alternative way of structuring the paragraph is to present a very general statement in the topic sentence that leads to the middle-level construct at the end of the paragraph. This structure, called "type II," is useful when the middle-level construct deserves special emphasis. An example follows:

> Jacob's school performance suggests that his difficulties may stem from either low general ability or poor academic skills. His IQ scores on the WISC-R (Verbal IQ = 123; Performance IQ = 125;

Full Scale IQ = 124), as well as his standard score equivalent on the PPVT-R (128), suggest that he functions in the superior range of general intellectual ability. By contrast, his academic achievement test scores on the Woodcock-Johnson Psycho-Educational Battery are much lower (Reading cluster standard score = 87; Mathematics = 83; Written Language = 82). These results suggest that Jacob may present an educationally significant specific learning disorder.

In this case, the focus of the paragraph is on the middle-level construct "specific learning disorder." Its position at the end of the paragraph gives it special emphasis because it is important new information about the child's functioning.

To summarize the elements of the two types of paragraphs:

Type I: 1. A *topic sentence* that includes a middle-level construct
2. *Data*
3. A *conclusion*, which usually summarizes and explains the functional significance of the findings

Type II: 1. A *topic sentence* without an middle-level construct
2. *Data*
3. A *conclusion* that includes and emphasizes a middle-level construct

Remember that the model stresses, first, the importance of establishing a particular kind of logical sequence in a report sentence or paragraph. You should move from a given, which provides the reader with a conceptual "anchor," to the new information provided by the writer. The model also stresses, second, the importance of referencing all middle-level constructs to data.

Examine the two types of paragraph structure from the point of view of the model. You can see that type I structure establishes a given-new sequence in its topic sentence. The data to which the model is tied follow it immediately as substantiation for the sequence. At a higher organizational level, type I structure supports the higher-level given-new sequence in the report's sections by moving from the referral question to recommendations sections and, thus, relates the paragraph's meaning to the sections of the report that follow it. The paragraph, once properly constructed, establishes information that creates a new shared referent, or given. This given then can be related to the new elements that follow it, such as additional related assessment data, conclusions, or recommendations.

Type II structure also follows the model's format. Here, the middle-level construct is not included in the topic sentence. The function of the topic sentence in this paragraph is only to establish the given. In this type of structure, all the new information is in the body of the paragraph that follows the given in the topic sentence. Data that follow the topic sentence lead to the concluding sentence in the paragraph that contains the middle-level construct.

This structure allows the author to emphasize the middle-level construct by inducing a minor degree of uncertainty in the reader, who is provided with data and reasoning, but not the actual conclusion until the end of the paragraph. This type of paragraph can be thought of as inducing an expectancy in the reader by providing the topic sentence and data; when the conclusion is provided, the expectancy is resolved. It can be hypothesized that the resolution of this expectancy is the means by which the paragraph causes the psychological experience of emphasis on the middle-level construct. The mechanism by which this occurs might be considered the written language equivalent of the more familiar experiments in perception, in which completion of a figure is demonstrated to produce the experience of completion in the viewer. (See Koffka, 1935, pp. 177-210.) The use of this type of structure to emphasize what is included at the end also is suggested by Strunk and White (1979, pp. 32-33).

In order to test the predictions of this model about paragraphs, a questionnaire was given to groups of clinical and counseling psychologists in a study of the model (Ownby, 1990a). The questionnaire included two sets of two paragraphs, one type I and the other type II structure. Each set of two paragraphs included one that conformed to the model and another that included the same elements, but was organized so that it did not conform to the model. For example, the topic sentence in the non-model type I paragraph was placed in the middle of the paragraph so that it did not establish a given prior to the inclusion of new data. In the non-model type II paragraph, the topic sentence and conclusion were placed together at the beginning of the paragraph so that it mirrored a more typical paragraph organization. Readers indicated that the paragraphs that conformed to the predictions of the model communicated more effectively than the matched non-model paragraphs.

Type I structures highlight the functional significance of test findings, while type II structures emphasize the MLC. In the example above about Sybil, the writer may know that the reader has some general awareness of her difficulties and will be most interested in an explanation of the relation between her emotional status and work performance. In the example above about the school child, Jacob may have been referred, as such children sometimes are, for behavior problems or emotional disturbance. Stressing the meaning of the middle-level construct in this case is an important way of making sure the reader understands that a problem that is not obvious to the casual observer may be the cause of Jacob's behavior. In the first instance, the larger given-new structure of the complete report is advanced by the conclusion of the paragraph, which establishes Sybil's depression as the reason for her adjustment difficulties; the fact that she is depressed becomes a shared referent between the writer and reader. The writer then can go on to elucidate etiological factors in Sybil's depression. In the second instance, the writer may go on to explain further the functional significance of Jacob's learning disorder, in this way again advancing the larger given-new structure of the complete report.

The Model with Sections of the Report

The model also may be applied to sections of the report. In this case, various givens can be connected to their respective new elements either directly or via middle-level constructs. For example, in the "Reason for Referral" section of the report, you might construct the following type I paragraph, which emphasizes the data:

In referring Jacob, Ms. Landsdowne, his first grade teacher, notes his frequent misbehavior. She reports that "he often talks out in class and acts in a way that is disruptive." Thus, the focus of this assessment was to determine what might account for Jacob's misbehavior in the classroom.

The general middle-level construct here is "misbehavior," while the substantiating data are quotes from Ms. Landsdowne's referral. The concluding statement summarizes the data and relates the paragraph to the report's overall purpose. In presenting background information, similar paragraphs might be written with concluding sentences that relate the information to the reason for referral.

A common practice is to begin the "Assessment Results" section of the report with a listing of assessment measures, in this way establishing what sources of information the writer has drawn from in developing the report. Depending on the method of reporting the results—by functional domain or hypotheses about the referral question—the succeeding paragraphs present data from the assessment measures. This structure follows the model by establishing the assessment measures as given elements before it discusses the new information, the assessment results.

The Results section, in turn, usually is followed by a Summary. The first paragraph of the summary almost always should be structured in type I format. Its given element should be (a) a phrase such as "Assessment results show . . . ," or (b) a brief restatement of the referral question. This allows the reader to relate the completed narration of assessment results that precede this section to the overall purpose of the assessment. Examples of these two approaches follow, with the given elements in italics:

a. *Assessment results show* that Sybil's work and school difficulties are probably the result of significant depression stemming from her parents' divorce approximately 6 months ago.

b. *The results show* that John is suffering from an anxiety disorder.

c. *Jacob's school behavior difficulties* probably stem from an educationally significant specific learning disorder.

The new element in these statements probably will be anticipated by the reader. The purpose of including this type of statement at this point in the report is to provide the reader with a bridge between the already narrated assessment results and the conclusions contained in the summary section.

As in other type I paragraphs, data that substantiate the generally phrased topic sentence follow, but in the summary this should consist of a brief review of significant assessment findings already discussed—no new data should be introduced in the summary. These review statements usually can be sentences that relate the middle-level constructs or assessment data introduced in the As- sessment Results section. They now are shared referents due to their having been related to data in previous statements. In Sybil's case, the topic sentence provided above could be followed by:

Her behavior during assessment, her reported low mood, and her responses to the MMPI all support this idea.

In John's case:

His complaints of panic and terror, as well as observations of him during an episode, suggest that this observation is correct.

In Jacob's case:

In the absence of other reasons for these difficulties, the severe discrepancy between his scores on measures of ability and achieve- ment supports this idea.

The final sentence in the Summary always should relate the con- clusions contained in the summary to the Recommendations sec- tion that will follow it. This sentence should include a given ele- ment that refers to the assessment results and a new element which is a general recommendation for a course of action. In Sybil's case, this might be:

These results indicate that psychotherapeutic interventions should be considered with Sybil.

In John's case:

These findings suggest the potential utility of medical and psychotherapeutic interventions with John.

In Jacob's case:

These results show that Jacob may be eligible for special educa- tional assistance.

The Recommendations section then follows, perhaps headed by a generally phrased given-new sequence such as "This assessment suggests that the following recommendations may be helpful to those who are working with this client." After this heading, detailed recommendations can be listed, such as, "Explore assertiveness training with Sybil" or "Try a linguistic approach to reading instruction with Jacob."

The Model and the Complete Report

This chapter has detailed how the central ideas of the model can be applied to the various types of structural problems in report writing. The model also can be applied to organizational variables in the report; the report format suggested in Chapter 6 follows the guidelines of the model and already is used widely. An outline for the overall structure of the report might state briefly the preliminary givens necessary to understanding the report's ultimate conclusions. These probably would include a statement of the client's identifying data, the reason for referral, and the sources of information used in the assessment. The new elements to be discussed include the test results, the middle-level constructs used to explain test results, conclusions, summary, and recommendations. These elements establish the superordinate given elements in the report: the client, the purpose of the assessment, and the assessment tools used. The new elements make the assessment results shared referents with the reader by relating assessment data to middle-level constructs and conclusions. When assessment results become shared referents, the resulting newly created givens can be used to develop further the argument of the overall report into conclusions and recommendations.

The Worksheet

The specificity of the model allows you to construct a report writing worksheet (Fig. 4). With this worksheet, you can make model sequences explicit even though raw assessment data, middle-level constructs, conclusions, and recommendations may appear in different sections. Note that the worksheet also can be organized by section of report, ability domain, or any other organizing principle you wish.

Once the macrostructure of the report is outlined with the model, the writing of the exposition can proceed easily. After background data and the reason for referral are presented, the content of the report narrative can be drawn directly from the model worksheet. Not all data elements must be written into the body of the report;

FIGURE 4

EXAMPLE OF AN EXPOSITORY PROCESS MODEL WORKSHEET

Domain	Data	MLC	Conclusion	Recommendation
Cognitive-Academic	1) Impulsive sight word recognition errors 2) WISC-R scores: Arithmetic = 6 Digit Span = 6 Coding = 4 3) Test behavior: Overactive	1) Attention 2) Distractibility 3) Impulsivity	1) Skills are poor 2) Possible attention deficit disorder	1) Provide structure in classroom 2) Provide reading instruction with "stop and think" approach 3) Refer for medical evaluation
Behavioral	1) Principal says: "Defiant" 2) Teacher says: "Can't control" 3) Rating scales: "Acting out"	1) Behavior disturbance	1) Possible conduct disorder	1) Possible special class placement 2) Reality therapy group 3) Community program for "predelinquents"

the writer should draw selected examples from the data column, always using at least one element for each middle-level construct that is linked to a shared referent and keeping in mind the intended recipient's knowledge of the middle-level constructs used in the report.

Additional examples for practice are provided in Appendix A.

Summary

The expository process model is the result of a synthesis of the ideas of psycholinguistic research on the given-new contract in discourse comprehension, Appelbaum's contribution of the idea of the middle-level construct, and of previous research on report writing. Through this synthesis, the model provides a model for structuring the elements of the psychological report. It gives guidance about how to write sentences, paragraphs, and the larger sections of the report. Several studies have shown that sentences and paragraphs written within the model's guidelines are viewed as significantly more credible and persuasive than similar sentences and paragraphs that are not written within the guidelines of the model.

There are several advantages to using the model: (a) it ensures that all statements are data-based, a characteristic recommended by many experts in the field; (b) it clarifies the logical structure of each argument in the report, from raw data to recommendations; (c) it provides a model to guide report writers; and (d) empirical support shows that it may be useful in achieving the goals of report writing. It is not a panacea for the ills of report writing—it will not cure problems in basic knowledge of assessment procedures nor will it cure problems that arise from an assessment that is poorly organized or thought out. Initially, its use even may appear to make the process of report writing more difficult, but with practice the model can help the psychologist write more readable and more useful reports.

5

REPORTING MODELS AND LINGUISTIC STYLES

This chapter discusses two important internal-organizational variables, model and style; the third organizational variable, format, is considered in Chapter 6. The way in which the sections of the report are organized and the general tone of the language used in the report are broad concerns of the writer. Here, the problem of organization will be termed *reporting model*, while the problem of general tone will be referred to as the problem of *style*. The two issues are closely related because both model and style depend on a determination of the precise function of the report in its context. You may recall that the theory of reporting presented in the introduction specifies that organizational variables interact with contextual variables: The report's model and style depend on the referral agent, problem, and environment.

The purpose of the report already has been defined as providing credible and persuasive statements about clients. A more specific consideration of the function of the report in its context will be necessary, however, in order to decide which reporting model to use. Two major models are current: *hypothesis-oriented*, in which the report is organized around the possible answers to the referral questions, and *domain-oriented*, in which the report is organized around a set of ability or functional domains. A third model, *test-oriented*, is organized around a test-by-test description of results, but is not as commonly used.

Your own beliefs about the nature of psychological assessment also should be considered in choosing the reporting model. For example, if you have a background in humanistic psychology, you might feel uncomfortable in writing a report that is organized around test results because you feel that this sort of report tends to reduce the client to a set of numbers. Another psychologist with extensive training in psychodynamic personality theory may find it difficult to organize the report in a manner inconsistent with his or her theory. Many psychologists have developed a personal style in report writing of which a particular model is an essential part. The author, therefore, may be reluctant to modify his or her style even though it might be desirable in order to better tailor the report for its function.

For example, a report written to a client's psychotherapist might attempt to provide, in addition to answers to specific questions, a general description of the client's personality and functioning. A report in forensic psychology, by contrast, might address a specific issue, such as a client's competency to stand trial. In the first case, the writer might write a domain-oriented report, while in the second the author might address only the hypothesis that the client is or is not competent to take part in legal proceedings.

The wishes of the report's intended recipient also may affect the choice of model. The psychotherapist mentioned above might be very interested in the additional data about the client provided in the domain-oriented report, while the judge or lawyer who reads the same report might find the additional material irrelevant to the purpose of the psychologists' assessment.

The relation of these issues to model choice is considered in this chapter. More detailed discussion of how to tailor the report to professional specialty and theoretical orientation is provided in Chapter 8.

Reporting Models

The term "models" primarily refers to the organization by which assessment data are presented in the report. Thus, models are most important to consider in writing the Assessment Results section of the report, though choice of model also may affect the way other sections, such as Reason for Referral or Background Information, are written. The three models to be discussed here are (a) hypothesis-oriented; (b) domain-oriented; and (c) test-oriented. While in practice it might be possible to identify other models, these three probably can be considered representative of classes of models overall.

Hypothesis-oriented. The hypothesis-oriented report provides the reader with a statement or series of statements about the answers the assessment can provide to the referral questions. The remainder of the sections can address specific issues related to the hypotheses by providing model-based paragraphs that communicate assessment results. The following example is drawn from a neuropsychological test report about a woman referred for evaluation of memory difficulties. Because of the report's length, only the first and second paragraphs of the Assessment Results section are reproduced here in order to illustrate how a general hypothesis can be stated and then followed with supporting information.

Results of this assessment indicate that there are probably multiple sources of Ms. Client's complaints and apparent difficulties. She shows quite obvious mental clouding, difficulties in new verbal learning, motor difficulties suggestive of left cerebral hemisphere dysfunction, and social-emotional difficulties; all of these may be related to her current adjustment problems.

Mental clouding and attentional difficulties were noted on interview with Ms. Client. She has frequent lapses as she speaks, loses her train of thought often, and requires prompting in order for her to remain on the topic . . . this problem alone would make it difficult for Ms. Client to function in any job that requires concentration, even at so rudimentary level as making mental arithmetic calculations. In this connection, it should be noted that Ms. Client performed particularly poorly on those subtests of the WAIS-R that require short-term memory (Digit Span = 4 forward and 3 backward) and mental problem solving (Arithmetic scaled score = 6, or the 9th percentile). In addition, she performed poorly on a subtest that involves concentration in combination with clerical speed and accuracy (Digit Symbol scaled score = 5, or the 5th percentile). These difficulties are likely to continue to interfere with Ms. Client's ability to function occupationally.

In assessment of her memory difficulties . . .

The report then continues with paragraphs that discuss Ms. Client's memory difficulties, possible left cerebral hemisphere dysfunction, and social-emotional difficulties. Each of the paragraphs discusses one of the issues raised in the hypotheses paragraph placed at the beginning of the section. Each paragraph addresses a specific concern raised in the Reason for Referral section. The Summary section then ties together the answers provided in each paragraph and provides an overview of the client's functioning.

Domain-oriented. The advantages of the domain-oriented model are its comprehensiveness and its ability to communicate a balanced picture of the client's strengths and weaknesses. The writer may organize the Results section with or without headings, depending on the complexity and length of the report. Useful headings might be Cognitive Abilities, Academic Achievement, or Personality Functioning. Within the sections defined by these headings, a narrative of test results can be written that focuses on providing a general description of the client and relating test data to the referral question. Paragraphs constructed within the guidelines of the EPM will serve this function.

A potential disadvantage of this model is the possibility that you will provide the reader with more information than he or she wishes. Use of this model is indicated when the report's intended recipient is likely to be interested in an extended discussion of the client's abilities and personality functioning. This situation might arise when the reason for referral is to obtain a better "general understanding" of the client. This model also might be appropriate when the referral request is vague, and it is not possible to obtain further clarification of the referring person's wishes with respect to the report. Here, the writer may provide the reader with as much information as is reasonable in the hope that he or she will answer the questions the referring person may have about the client. The relation of referral problem to type of assessment and report is discussed further in Chapter 6.

Here is an example of a domain-oriented report's Assessment Results section. Headings are used that reflect specific domains of function.

Cognitive abilities. Results of this assessment indicate that Marie is probably functioning in the average range of general intellectual ability (WISC-R Verbal IQ = 103; Performance IQ = 100; Full Scale IQ = 101). When Marie's scores on the subtests of the WISC-R are combined so that they contribute to specific abilities (factor analytically derived deviation quotients), she shows borderline impaired performance on the factor that represents attention, concentration, and control of high-level cognitive processes. This score suggests that Marie may present difficulties in sustaining attention in a large classroom and that her teachers may report that she often must be reminded to pay attention. Other children who score at this level often have academic skills difficulties and specific learning disorders.

Visual-motor abilities. Assessment of Marie's visual-motor abilities as her skill at copying geometric forms with pencil and paper . . .

Academic achievement. Assessment of Marie's reading and math skills (Woodcock-Johnson Psycho-Educational Battery) suggests that while she performs at average levels in the area of reading skills development, she may perform at lower levels in the area of math skills (Reading cluster standard score = 99, or the 48th percentile; Math cluster standard score = 90, or the 26th percentile) . . .

This report shows how the domain-oriented report can provide a complete and thorough understanding of the areas of the client's functioning evaluated during the assessment.

Test-oriented. In this model, assessment results are presented sequentially by assessment measure used, often with headings such as, "Wechsler Adult Intelligence Scale – Revised" or "Minnesota Multiphasic Personality Inventory." Although this model has the advantage of making the sources of assessment data clear, it has little else to recommend it. The emphasis on tests detracts from the overall presentation of the client as a person by drawing attention to specific tests and scores rather than to their relevance to the client's functioning. The emphasis on tests also communicates the impression that psychological assessment consists of giving tests and interpreting them on an individual basis, rather than using multiple information sources in order to arrive at answers to important questions about the client. Although popular in the past, this model is to be avoided.

Each of the reporting models has advantages and disadvantages. Exclusive use of the hypothesis-oriented model means that occasionally you may not supply the reader with all the information he or she wants, but, conversely, exclusive use of the domain-oriented model may mean that you spend time unnecessarily reporting data that the reader isn't interested in knowing. Ultimately, then, the decision of what report model to use should depend on how the report is to function within the contextual variables.

Linguistic Style

Elsewhere, Fred Wallbrown and I (Ownby & Wallbrown, 1986) defined style in psychological reports as "the consistent tone of the language of the report defined by vocabulary and the complexity and type of grammatic structure used" (p. 32). This definition implies, first, that the writer of the report makes certain reasoned decisions about the way he or she uses language in the report. Most writers of psychological reports, for example, won't use slang or idiom because such use would be inconsistent with the professional tone of the psychological report. A second implication of this definition is that the writer's decisions are made on a consistent basis over time. The choices of vocabulary and grammatic structure are likely to be the same at the end of the report as at the beginning. Third, this definition divides style into two closely related elements: vocabulary and grammatic structure. This division will make consideration of the types of decisions writers make in producing a report easier in this discussion. With this definition in mind, it may be useful to consider what experts on report writing have suggested.

Klopfer (1960) provides an early, but still pertinent discussion of style in psychological reports. He reviews research to the date of his writing and concludes that reports should be written in a style that emphasizes accuracy, integration, readability, clarity, and individuality. Klopfer also stresses the importance of adherence to the rules of basic English prose in writing clear and easily understood reports. Perhaps his most specific statement about style is the following: "It is my contention that any statement found in psychological reports could be made comprehensible to any literate individual of at least average intelligence" (p. 58). By inference from these statements, it appears that Klopfer believes that reports should be written with a minimum of technical vocabulary and in a manner that places readability ahead of other grammatic concerns.

In another early discussion, Huber (1961) admonishes the writer to develop his or her own style. Huber suggests that "report writing is to some degree an art in the sense that the writer's personality and outlook are imposed on the data . . . Style of writing is one of the means by which a writer imposes his personality on a report" (p. 81). He goes on to say that "you should resist anyone's imposing a style on you" (p. 81). Huber thus emphasizes the personal nature of the choices the writer must make in developing style and apparently suggests that the writer's own interest in developing a style is the primary method by which a personal style can evolve.

Tallent (1976) identifies three styles of writing in reports: scientific, literary, and journalistic. The scientific style might mimic the objectivity of the write-up of a laboratory experiment and, thereby, imply a degree of scientific accuracy. An example of this style might be: "These test scores and observations confirm the hypothesis that the child is emotionally labile due to the home situation." A literary style might use multiple modifiers even to the point of exaggeration with the intention of conveying a vivid picture of the client: "The child's outrageous behavior derives from the appalling home situation and the unfortunate child's enormous difficulty in coping with it." A journalistic style attempts to convey a maximum amount of information succinctly by relying on short sentences and commonplace vocabulary: "The behavior that is giving the teacher trouble is caused by the child's problems at home." Aspects of each of these styles have a place in certain contexts; situations occasionally may merit the expressiveness of the literary style, the erudition of the scientific style, or the bluntness of the journalistic style.

Hollis and Donn (1979) state that, "the best stylistic approach in preparing the psychological report is to endeavor to be clear, simple, concise, orderly, and developmental" (p. 122). They go on to list several rules for style and state that the report should reflect clearly the individuality of the client about whom it is written rather than use stereotyped terms or phrases that might be applicable to any number of clients. They argue that conclusions should be advanced "as straightforwardly as the validity and reliability data and information will permit" (p. 123). Hollis and Donn note that the writer's preference should be for writing short words, short sentences, and short paragraphs. They suggest that each paragraph should contain just one main thought. Thus, these authors advocate a style that emphasizes simple vocabulary and grammatic constructions.

Another source on style worth consideration is the *Publication Manual of the American Psychological Association*, which serves as a standard in many areas of psychology. The authors of the *Manual* emphasize the need for orderly presentation of ideas, smoothness of expression, economy of expression, and precision in word choice. They note with respect to sentence length that "although writing only in short, simple sentences produces choppy and boring prose, writing exclusively in long, involved sentences creates difficult, sometimes incomprehensible material. Varied sentence length helps readers maintain interest and comprehension" (1983, p. 34). They make the point about vocabulary and grammatic structure in a way that provides an illustration: "Direct, declarative sentences with simple, common words are usually best" (p. 34). Finally, the authors of the *Manual* suggest that paragraph length also be varied: "Single-sentence paragraphs may be abrupt. Paragraphs that are too long . . . are likely to lose the reader's attention. New paragraphs provide a pause for the reader – a chance to store one step in the conceptual development before beginning another" (p. 34). The authors of the *Manual* provide recommendations similar to those of several other authors in suggesting the need for simple and direct communication. They make the additional recommendation, however, that vocabulary and grammatic structure should vary in order to make what is written more interesting to the reader.

The Professional Style

As with other areas of report writing already reviewed, it can be said on the issue of style that although there is no adequate body of research at present that would allow firm recommendations about style, a consensus can be drawn from what authorities have suggested. The style suggested by this consensus will be termed the *professional style*, which emphasizes that it is not literary or journalistic, but a style that is appropriate to the communication of important information derived from technical procedures. Its elements can be summarized as follows:

1. In the area of *vocabulary choice*, the writer who is using the professional style will choose words that have these characteristics:
   - common usage ("widespread" rather than "prevalent")
   - shortness ("skill" rather than "competency")
   - inclusion in standard general reference works (not technical vocabulary)
   - precise meaning (have a specific use with a clear significance)

2. In the area of grammatic structure, the writer will choose a variety of sentence constructions and lengths and will use different types as appropriate to the content to help the reader maintain interest in the writing.

3. At the level of paragraph structure, the writer will tend to keep paragraphs short and focused on a single concept. Similar, but related concepts will be contained in separate paragraphs that are physically close to each other and that are related by concluding and topic sentences.

There are several advantages to this formulation of style. It is consistent with what virtually every authority on writing in psychology suggests, yet it is flexible enough to give writers freedom to develop a personally effective mode of expression. It is neither overly prescriptive nor so vague as to be useless as a guide for the writer. In addition, it goes beyond exhortations to use simple words and sentences in written communication and recognizes that writers should vary word choice and sentence length in order to avoid monotony. Whether a word or usage satisfies these three criteria can be checked; if the writer is in doubt about whether word choice or grammatic structure is consistent with professional style, he or she can refer to the three elements listed.

Examples can illustrate this. In the area of vocabulary, the writer might be unsure whether a word such as "arduous" is appropriate for use in a report to be sent to a social worker in a community agency. Tests suggested above were commonness and shortness.

Therefore, the writer should determine whether there is a more common or shorter word, as for instance by consulting a dictionary of synonyms. Although arduous is a word in standard English, "difficult" is more commonly used and is probably to be preferred in writing a psychological report. Similar tests can be devised for determining whether writing is consistent with other elements of professional style.

Some Common Problems

Although an exhaustive catalog of stylistic problems is beyond the scope of this book, some problems are unique to psychological report writing and are discussed here. If you are concerned with stylistic problems in general, you might refer to Strunk and White's (1979) classic *The Elements of Style*. Few short books do a better job of discussing basic principles of writing. The *Publication Manual of the American Psychological Association* (American Psychological Association, 1983) also provides a discussion of specific style problems encountered in psychological writing, although much of it deals with writing about research investigations. What follows, then, is a listing of some common problems specific to report writing with suggested solutions.

Perhaps the most common stylistic problem specific to report writing is the author's failure to keep in mind the difference between the client and the client's test scores. For example:

> POOR: The client was in the average range of ability.
> BETTER: The client's score fell in the average range.

Here, the writer must keep in mind that test scores describe aspects of the client's functioning, but do not define the person. The same principle arises when one is discussing a diagnosis:

> POOR: The mentally retarded often require close supervision. Psychotics sometimes recover completely.
> BETTER: Mentally retarded persons often require close supervision. Persons with psychotic symptoms sometimes recover completely.
> EVEN BETTER: Persons with low levels of general intellectual ability and adaptive behavior deficits often require close supervision. Persons who have difficulties with reality testing and have disabling social skills deficits sometimes recover completely.

In these examples, the writer can emphasize the important distinction between a diagnosis and the person given the diagnosis. In the examples labeled "Even Better," the writer has gone beyond this distinction to provide concrete examples of the types of problems that impair these persons' functioning. Although this approach requires more words, it may have the effect of encouraging the reader to think about the client as a unique individual with certain problems in living. If these problems in living are addressed specifically in the recommendations, the reader may be more optimistic about his or her ability to help the client. It may be recalled that Sudduth's (1976) study, reviewed in Chapter 2, suggests precisely this.

A common complaint of readers of psychological reports is that writers hedge their statements with too many modifiers:

> POOR: It appears at least somewhat possible that the client may develop a potentially more serious disorder.
> BETTER: The client may develop a more serious disorder.

Notice that the second example preserves the author's intent to signal to the reader that the outcome "develop a more serious disorder" is only a possibility—but one that merits concern. A similar problem can be encountered in reporting test scores:

> POOR: These test results suggest the possibility that the client may be only mildly disabled.
> BETTER: These test results show that the client may be only mildly disabled.

Here again, the second sentence still preserves a degree of doubt appropriate when results do not allow greater certainty.

Another problem in this area is the need for writers to qualify judiciously statements with words such as "suggest," "may indicate," or "may show" when assessment data cannot be interpreted validly with more confidence. The writer should keep in mind that the relation between any psychological test score and the client's later behavior is only a probability. Although there may be a very great likelihood that a person with certain test scores will display particular behaviors, the writer should qualify predictions about the client's current and future function when predicted behaviors have not been observed directly. On the other hand, when the author has observed behaviors or obtained test scores directly, the more vigorous active voice should be used. The following examples show this distinction, with the verbs and qualifiers in italics:

Results of this assessment *indicate* that the client *continues to show* a number of behaviors and thought processes characteristic of schizophrenia. Results thus *suggest* that although at present she is functioning well, ongoing monitoring by mental health professionals *may be required* for her to continue to function at this level.

Here, the writer makes clear the difference between facts known with reasonable certainty (behaviors and thought processes) and predictions based only on probabilities, by appropriate qualification of the words used to discuss the client. This practice should be differentiated from the inappropriate hedging illustrated above.

Here is another example, in this instance one that deals with reporting test results:

Ability testing *indicates* that Martha is *probably functioning* in the low average range of general intellectual ability.

Some authors might quarrel with the word "probably" in this sentence and might suggest that the test result shows conclusively that Martha's intellectual functioning is in the low average range. This interpretation of test scores is not precise, however, because many factors could have intervened to prevent Martha from scoring higher. If the author of this report were required to testify about the assessment in court, for example, the statement "probably functioning" would be defensible under cross-examination because the psychologist has only stated that the test score may indicate something about the client. A statement made with absolute certainty would be difficult to defend.

Once he or she appreciates this distinction, the writer should strive to make it equally clear to the reader. If there is uncertainty in an observation, the writer should not be subtle in communicating this fact to the reader. If reasonable certainty exists about a statement, a direct statement should be made. At times, additional information can help to clarify this issue, as in the following example:

POOR: The client appeared nervous during test administration.

BETTER: The client's behavior, such as nervous smiles, trembling hands, and a tentative approach to tasks, suggests that he was nervous during assessment.

You may notice that the second statement conforms to the guidelines of the model, while the first does not. Here the model can help you to deal with this problem.

One final stylistic issue: It is essential that the author of a report, no less than authors in other contexts in psychology, avoid the use of language or expressions that indicate ethnic or sexual stereotyping. Consideration of examples of these problems is provided at length in the *Publication Manual* (American Psychological Association, 1983, pp. 43-49); if you are unsure of the appropriate way to express what you wish to say, you should consult the *Manual*.

The purpose of this discussion of style is to help you learn ways to communicate the results of your assessments more effectively. Beyond these general guidelines about vocabulary and structure, you may wish to consult one of the style manuals suggested above. A final comment on style was provided by Taylor and Teicher, writing more than 45 years ago. It is still relevant today:

> The writer need not be overly concerned with making . . . [the] report "professional." A studied attempt at being "professional" or at being "scientific" not only robs the psychological reporting of the dynamic qualities which distinguish a human relationship from an experiment with test tubes, but, more seriously, invariably reflects a basic attitude in the psychologist which will prevent . . . [him or her] from establishing a warm, genuine, friendly rapport (1946, p. 332).

Improving Writing Style

You can work to improve your style by doing several things when you write. Using the materials in Appendices A, B, and C will help you to learn how to use the expository process model and diagnose problems in the reports you already write. Just using the model, perhaps by filing out the worksheets provided in Chapter 4, will help create a more concise and logical organization for the reports you write; in addition, it will be based in the raw data of the assessment. If you follow the guidelines provided above on vocabulary choice and grammatic structure, you should be able to write reports in sections that encourage the reader to find out what is contained in them rather than overwhelming the reader with a page-length paragraph.

The *Publication Manual of the American Psychological Association* (American Psychological Association, 1983) also includes suggestions for improving your writing (pp. 35-36). The authors of the *Manual* suggest that you write from an outline, put a draft aside and return to it after a day or two, and then ask a colleague to read it and give you feedback about it. These are all excellent ways to obtain a fresh perspective on your writing, for when you work on something intently it is easy to become so immersed in it that you lose your objectivity. Things which are obviously unclear or awkward on a rereading may have seemed completely correct earlier. Working from an outline might seem to require additional effort, but, in fact, it can reduce the ultimate work by streamlining the process of writing the final draft. Organizing your thoughts by means of an outline is one way to make sure that you know what you want to write, and when you know what you want to write, you are far less likely to become entangled in a stylistic morass later on; as Woodford (1967) has suggested, there may be a close relation between clear writing and clear thinking.

You also should recognize that economical and clear expression in report writing is not a goal that, once attained, can be ignored in favor of more interesting pursuits. Learning to write well must be a continuing process in which you obtain feedback about your writing and modify it on the basis of the information received. Feedback can be of the formal type suggested by Ownby and Wallbrown (1983), or you can give yourself feedback by rereading reports after an interval or by asking colleagues for feedback about what you have written. More suggestions for improving your reports are contained in Appendix B. These are valuable ways of developing a more readable and effective style.

Summary

This chapter has reviewed common problems in choice of reporting model and writing style. Problems with reporting model usually stem from a failure to consider the purpose of the report and the needs of the reader. Several models were reviewed, and suggestions for the use of each were made. Only a few specific recommendations about style were presented. In general, the specifics of style have been left to the writer to learn for him- or herself because learning style is, in part, the same as learning to write — and this book cannot serve that function. It is also because style cannot be learned in a mechanical way, though devices such as the expository process model can help. Style must be developed through the interaction of writer preferences and the demands of the assessment task. For these reasons, you are encouraged to use the techniques suggested for improving your writing and to consult an authoritative reference whenever necessary. In this way, your style can both become better in the specific instance and at the same time develop over a period of time into a more effective tool for communication.

6

THE REPORT IN CONTEXT

This chapter discusses the need for tailoring the report to its context and suggests ways of making the report most effective in the situation into which it is sent. Throughout this book, the need for writing reports that are made individual with respect to the client and the client's situation has been stressed; in this chapter, you are given specifics about how to make reports individual and appropriate to their contexts. The dimensions of contexts are discussed, ways to assess each dimension are presented, and ways for you to modify your writing style are suggested, based on your assessment of the report's context. Prior to any substantial consideration of the context of the report, however, it will be necessary to consider how to develop an overall concept for the report.

Developing the Overall Concept

The importance of developing an overall concept for a report is emphasized by several authorities, including Klopfer (1960) and Huber (1961). Klopfer, for example, suggests that lack of focus is a common problem: "Inexperienced and poorly trained psychologists have a tendency to put together an indigestible mass of discreet observations and a 'cook book' list of signs and indicators without any sort of overview or attempt to apply these to the problems which prompted the original referral" (p. 7). Huber, as does Klopfer, devotes an entire chapter to the topic. Hollis and Donn (1979, p. 20) have echoed this idea more recently.

If the consensus of authorities is that the writer should establish an overall concept or formulation for the assessment report, how, you might legitimately ask, is this task to be carried out? The simplest and probably the best way of developing an overall concept for the report is to define clearly the questions addressed by the assessment and respond to them briefly. If you are writing an hypothesis-oriented report, a statement of the answers to the assessment questions can serve as the first paragraph of the Assessment Results sections, while if you are writing a domain-oriented report, the answers can be supplied in the sections where they are most relevant to the data. The form illustrated in Figure 5 can be used in this process; in conjunction with the expository process model worksheet (Figure 4 in Chapter 4) the two forms constitute a complete outline of the report to be written.

Examples will once again, it is hoped, clarify these issues. Take the case of Mr. Fiduciary, a forty-five-year-old man who was referred by his physician because he complains of being constantly tired (without physical basis) and of lacking the energy to work in his successful accounting business. Test results show high scores on

FIGURE 5
ASSESSMENT QUESTIONS AND ANSWERS

Questions	Answers
1) What is the reason for Mr. Fiduciary's lack of energy?	1) Mr. Fiduciary is depressed.
2) What can be done about it?	2) a. Provide psychotherapy b. Try antidepressants

MR. FIDUCIARY'S MODEL WORKSHEET

Data	Middle-level Construct	Conclusion	Recommendations
Complains "tired" Has lost weight Sleep disturbance High scale 2	Depression	is present:	Provide psychotherapy Try antidepressants

scale 2 of the MMPI (this probably indicates depression); interview with the man reveals that he has lost about 15 pounds during the last three months and that he often wakes up early in the morning and can't get back to sleep. The man does not, however, complain of low mood, but interview also reveals that he and his wife were divorced about six months ago and that he has distant relations with his children and other family members. He lives alone. Thus, the assessment data clearly suggest that the man is depressed (the middle-level construct in the expository process model worksheet illustrated in the lower portion of Figure 5). Assessment data are referenced to this construct, the only one that will be discussed at present.

The referral problem in the top portion of Figure 5 is listed in the Problems and Questions section as the referring physician might have stated it, although perhaps the psychologist will have made it more direct and rendered it as a question: "What is the reason for Mr. Fiduciary's lack of energy?" In addition, the implicit question "What can be done about it?" is added because it is quite likely that the physician will want an opinion about what should be done to help Mr. Fiduciary, even if the physician does not say so explicitly. The answers to the problem are listed in the "Answers" section: "The client is depressed," "He's depressed because he believes he has no reason to live," "Attempt to involve the client in therapy," and "Suggest a trial of antidepressant medication" (if you know the physician will welcome advice on this sort of issue).

When you are writing the actual report, then, you might draw the Reason for Referral section directly from the form and say something such as, "Mr. Fiduciary was referred by his physician, Dr. B. Pressure, for evaluation of his difficulties with constant feelings of tiredness that have interfered with his ability to work." The Background Information section of the report can be written from the personal history data listed on the expository process model worksheet. It's important to remember to write this section from the model worksheet rather than from notes because writing from the worksheet ensures that all of the interview data you include will be related to the central focus of the report. If you write from your notes, you may include interesting bits of information about the client that are unrelated to the assessment questions.

If you write a hypothesis-oriented report, as might be appropriate when responding to a specific question posed by a physician, you could write the first paragraph of the Assessment Results question from the Answers section of the form. In the case of Mr. Fiduciary, this might be a brief paragraph:

Results of this assessment suggest that the reason for Mr. Fiduciary's persistent feelings of tiredness and difficulties in working is that he is depressed. Test results and information obtained on interview support this idea; interview data also indicate possible reasons why Mr. Fiduciary may be depressed.

This paragraph could be followed by a series of paragraphs, each of which deals with a separate issue, such as evidence for Mr. Fiduciary being depressed, the life events that surround him that may have caused it, and how Mr. Fiduciary views his current life situation.

In this way, the two forms, Assessment Questions and Answers (top of Figure 5) and the Expository Process Model Worksheet (Figure 4 in Chapter 4 and bottom of Figure 5), provide structure that allows you to develop an overall concept of the assessment. With this concept, writing the rest of the report will be much easier, and it is almost certain that you will not simply give the reader "an indigestible mass of discreet observations" (Klopfer, 1960, p. 7). Practice in using the two forms will allow you to develop the skill of determining the overall concept of the report. With this method of determining the overall concept in mind, we now can turn to consideration of how the report, once conceptualized, is to function in its context.

Assessment of Context

In reviewing what authorities have written about reports, we have seen repeatedly that almost all emphasize the need to tailor the report to its context. The process of tailoring involves manipulating the internal-organizational variables of style, format, and model to write a report that you are certain the reader will be able to understand and use. This change in style will not be limited, however, to using or not using certain terms, but will include tailoring your use of vocabulary and grammatic structure to the characteristics of the report's intended reader, the assessment problem, and the environment in which the report will function. Within each of these dimensions of context, other areas on which the dimension can be rated can be specified, which will provide a way to examine the context of the assessment in detail. These other areas for understanding the external-contextual variables are discussed in the following sections.

Assessing the referral agent. In this discussion, it is assumed that the report's intended reader is the same person who made the original referral for evaluation. The areas on which this dimension can be assessed are (a) professional affiliation of the referral source; (b) level of training of the referral source; and (c) complexity of the referral source. The meaning of the first two of these dimensions may be obvious; the third deals with the occasionally ambiguous motivations of the referral agent as he or she functions within the broader context of a system, such as a hospital, school, or agency.

It is important to consider the professional affiliation of the referral source prior to writing the referral. Reports written for a physician, attorney, psychologist, teacher, or social worker may differ from each other in format, model, and style. The report to a physician, for example, about a specific referral question might be in the form of a short letter in the hypothesis-oriented model, that reports only a summary account of the assessment and its implications for client treatment, while the report to a special education teacher about the same problem might be three to four pages long (or longer) in a domain-oriented report. (For more on this issue, see Chapter 7.)

Here is an example of two reports written about the same child, referred for evaluation because of an unusually high activity level and problems in paying attention in class. The first report is to the pediatric neurologist who referred the child for evaluation. The neurologist knows the psychologist both personally and professionally, an aspect of the situation that affects the tone of the language (it is more informal for a person known to the psychologist), the amount of raw data included in the report (the neurologist knows and trusts the psychologist's statements on the basis of past experience), and even the closing used in the letter—"cordially" rather than "sincerely."

Dear Dr. Neuro,

I saw your patient, Billy Active (DOB: 10-8-85), on your referral for evaluation of his difficulties with a high activity level and problems in paying attention in class. Results of my assessment show that Billy probably displays an unusually high activity level (suggested both by his teacher's responses to the Conners Rating Scale and my observations of him in the office) and significant problems in attending in the large group situation.

Billy's scores on subtests of the WISC-R that require attention were particularly low (for example, Digit Span subtest scaled score = 4, or the 2nd percentile; Coding subtest scaled score = 5, or the 5th percentile). These scores are in contrast to Billy's performances on both verbal and nonverbal subtests, which were uniformly in the high average to superior range (for example, Vocabulary scaled score = 15, or the 95th percentile).

Overall, these results suggest that Billy presents a clear case of Attention-Deficit Hyperactivity Disorder and they would certainly support a trial of stimulant medication to determine whether it can be helpful in managing Billy's difficulties. I would recommend that Billy be reassessed in nine months to a year in order to monitor his progress in acquiring academic skills and that his response to medication, if you elect to try this route, be monitored by his teacher through the ongoing use of a rating scale such as the Conners.

> Cordially,
> Childe Psychologist

The following is an excerpt from a more lengthy report supplied to the special education teacher who is working with Billy. He or she is more likely to be interested in details of the behavioral assessment and in suggestions for instructional and behavioral management of the child in both large class and small group settings:

PSYCHOLOGICAL REPORT

Name: Billy Active   *DOB:* 10-8-85
Address: Suburbantown, State   *Date seen:* 1-5-91
                    Psychologist:
                       C. Psychologist, Ph.D

Reason for Referral

Billy was referred for evaluation by Dr. Neuro, his pediatric neurologist. Dr. Neuro requested evaluation of Billy's high level of activity and his reported difficulties in paying attention in the classroom.

Background Information

[This section would include relevant medical and personal history data about Billy. It might also include results of previous psychological and speech pathology evaluations carried out by the school and other agencies.]

Assessment Results

Sources of information

Wechsler Intelligence Scale for Children—Revised (WISC-R)
Woodcock-Johnson Psycho-Educational Battery (WJPEB)

•

•

•

[Other assessment measures would be listed here.]
Conners Pupil Rating Scale (Conners) completed by
Ms. Landsdowne, Billy's regular classroom teacher

Results of this assessment show that Billy probably is functioning in the high average range of general intellectual ability (WISC-R Verbal IQ = 118; Performance IQ = 109; Full Scale IQ = 114). Billy's scores on subtests of the WISC-R that require attention and sustained concentration, however, were much lower than these overall indices of his intellectual functioning. For example, on a measure of his ability to remember sequences of orally presented digits, his score was at the 2nd percentile (Digit Span subtest), while his score on a measure of rapid manipulation of symbols — entering small geometric symbols according to a numbered key — was at the 5th percentile (Coding subtest). Children who score at these levels on these subtests often are described as having difficulties in sustaining attention in the large classroom environment and are seen by others as having a short attention span and possible problems in learning.

•

•

•

[Other assessment results might be explained here.]

Assessment of Billy's reading skills suggests that although his reading achievement overall is not significantly below that expected for his age or estimated ability (WJPEB standard score for reading cluster = 108), he may have developed some poor strategies in reading which could be addressed in reading instruction. For example, on a sight word recognition task, Billy tended to rely on an impulsive strategy in which he only scanned the initial and final consonants before responding. Thus, he easily might confuse the words "cat" and "cut" because they differ only in their medial vowels . . . [Additional data about Billy's reading skills would be discussed here.]

Assessment of Billy's behavioral functioning through behavioral rating scale (Conners), observation, and parent and teacher report suggests that his general activity level is far higher than that of most children his age. It may be noted also that Billy's behavior is usually not well-directed or organized and can at times become frustrating to him as well as to those around him . . . [Additional information about Billy's behavior might be inserted here.]

•

•

•

[Additional assessment information is reported here.]

Summary and Recommendations

Results of this assessment show that Billy probably displays an unusually high level of activity along with educationally important difficulties in sustaining attention. It also can be noted that these difficulties are probably more severe in the large classroom setting than in the small group tutoring or one-to-one testing situations. . .

The following recommendations may be useful to those working with Billy:

1. It probably would be helpful for those who are working with Billy to arrange a cuing system with him to help remind him

to pay attention in class. A nonverbal cue, such as a hand sign, might be an effective cue for Billy and at the same time would keep to a minimum the potentially negative effects of giving him attention for problematic behavior. Giving him attention for his nonattending behavior might have the effect of making it more likely to occur.

2.   In reading work with Billy, it might be useful to encourage him to adopt a more reflective strategy in word recognition tasks, both in isolation and in context. He might be encouraged to say something such as "stop and think" to himself before he responded about a word. It also might be useful to encourage Billy directly to scan the middle of words before responding because it is with this aspect of word recognition skills that he has the most obvious difficulties.

3.   Medical evaluation for possible use of stimulant medication as part of a coordinated plan of behavioral and educational interventions for dealing with Billy's high activity level is indicated.

Although the second report is somewhat schematic, it quickly can be seen that it contains substantially more specific information about the child in question. The physician is primarily interested in knowing whether the psychologist thinks Billy is hyperactive and what the educational and medical implications of the problem may be. Depending on the physician, he or she may be interested in a statement of the potential usefulness of medication, although such a recommendation should be included only when the psychologist is certain that it will be welcomed — physicians vary widely in their interest even in suggestions from other health care professionals. In this case, Dr. Psychologist knew Dr. Neuro and was able to treat the subject of Billy's behavior briefly and informally. By contrast, Dr. Psychologist's report for the school is more detailed in providing specifics of test data, in which the teacher is likely to have an interest, as well as in detailing how the test and observational data relate to Billy's school behavior. The formal recommendations section provides specific techniques that the teacher could implement in large and small group settings for dealing with Billy's attention and behavior problems. Note that Billy's behavioral difficulty with impulsivity already intrudes into his reading skills and that Dr.

Psychologist has included suggestions for preventing Billy from becoming worse in this area.

The question of style with various referral sources is less clear, but can be addressed on the basis of level of professional training. The style of a report written about a client who is schizophrenic for a physician with specialized training in psychiatry, for example, will be quite different from that of a similar report written for a social worker in a public welfare agency. This is true because the two readers vary widely in the amount of background information they probably possess and their needs for information about the client are different. The psychiatrist may be interested in detailed and technical information about the client's mental status as he or she adjusts the client's medication for optimal effect, while the social worker may be most interested in a general statement about the client's functioning that will be helpful in establishing the client's disability for the purpose of obtaining financial support from government sources. Here, you can see that level of training and profession interact; the psychiatrist probably will receive the more detailed and more technical report, and the social worker will receive the less detailed and less technical report.

The assessment of the complexity of the referral source is a task that requires both diplomacy and insight. At the outset, it should be acknowledged that the referrer's own needs and feelings, as well as the interests of the client referred, enter into the decision to make a referral for evaluation. The situations that are the most difficult for the psychologist to influence are often those in which the motivations of the referral agent are complex and impinge upon the client's situation. Successful completion of the report requires as clear an understanding as possible of why the referral was made. The dimensions by which the referring agent can be assessed in this area are the complexity and openness of the agent's agenda in referring the client for evaluation. An example of simple and open agenda might be when a client in a medical hospital is referred for evaluation prior to some form of treatment. The referring agent, usually a physician, will want baseline information about the client's cognitive and emotional functioning prior to initiating treatment, such as radiation for treatment of cancer, in order to evaluate its possible effects. A complex and hidden agenda referral might occur in a community agency when a staff therapist and his or her supervisor disagree on an appropriate course of action for a client. The therapist might refer the client for evaluation in the hope that the psychologist's opinion will bolster the therapist's point of view. Here, the psychologist risks becoming ensnared in a disagreement between two other parties. The psychologist can play a useful role in such a situation, but risks alienating one or both parties in the struggle if the report doesn't address the referral questions in a diplomatic way.

There is perhaps some irony in the fact that assessment of this aspect of the referral process may be at once the least directly related to the client's needs, but at the same time the most important in the psychologist's professional success in establishing an influential relation with the referral agent. This is a critical step in helping the agent modify his or her approach to working with the client. The psychologist's success in this effort has a great impact on how his or her recommendations are viewed and the degree to which they are implemented. To complicate the problem further, the referral agent may not even be aware of, or at least not willing to acknowledge, his or her motivations.

The referral agent's motivations in making a referral can be understood as consisting of open, or acknowledged, and hidden, or unacknowledged, agendas. The referral agent's open agenda includes whatever public statement he or she makes about the reason for the referral, such as a request for guidance in planning treatment for a client, in helping a child learn to read, or in determining the fitness of a potential employee for a position. The agent's referral request also might be accompanied by requests for additional information, such as a general description of the client's personality, information about behavioral management strategies likely to be useful with a child, or the potential employee's likelihood of success in a higher-level position. Most referrals come to the psychologist with this sort of open agenda, prompted by the referral agent's sincere desire to help the client function well.

For various reasons, however, the referral agent's agenda may be partially hidden. One case in which a referral source may not openly acknowledge his or her interests when making the referral is when he or she is aware that the psychologist's help may be useful, but perceives that accepting the help is an indication of personal failure in working with client. Such persons may request the psychologist's assistance, but then be reluctant to try any of the recommendations developed from the assessment results. In addition, interventions that the agent may be persuaded to try often will fail in this situation, perhaps because of the agent's limited motivation in making them work. In extreme cases, the agent may simultaneously acknowledge that an evaluation was requested, but deny the need for help subsequent to the evaluation, even in the face of objective indications that such help is needed.

Another case in which the referral agent might have a partially hidden agenda arises in school psychology settings in which a teacher is discouraged about his or her ability to deal with a child and wishes the child to be placed in a special education classroom. The teacher ostensibly may ask the psychologist for assistance in helping the child to function in the educational environment, but in reality the teacher wants the psychologist's test data to help justify the removal of the child from the classroom. Here, the school psychologist's task is formidable in using both report and consultation to persuade the teacher to try new ways of helping the child.

Yet another problem that involves both open and hidden agendas, already alluded to above, is when two persons disagree on the nature of the client's problem or the steps required to deal with it. In this instance, the psychologist may be asked to evaluate in the hope that the psychologist's data will support one side of an argument that, at times, can be unrelated to a determination of the client's welfare. Although it is not always possible for the consulting psychologist to be aware that this sort of situation exists, when unsure the psychologist often can be of greatest service to the client by providing an honest opinion on the best course of action for the client, even when this opinion may run counter to that of other persons who are working with the client. Regardless of the political involvements, the psychologist's first duty is always to the welfare of the client. The psychologist cannot allow external circumstances to influence his or her report on a client until this obligation is fulfilled (albeit as tactfully as possible).

Assessing the referral problem. Many reports are not written in as satisfactory a fashion as possible because the psychologist does not adequately determine the nature of the referral problem prior to writing. It is not possible to write the report of a problem-oriented assessment if the problem and its relation to the environment variables are not specified clearly. A learning problem with a child, for example, might be a teacher's primary concern in referring a child, but the alert psychologist should assess the child's behavior in other contexts as well as look for clues about how the child's behavior may be related to the observed learning problem.

One way of making a more detailed assessment of the problem is to arrange a formal or informal conference with the referral agent prior to initiating assessment activities. This sort of assessment might be formal in situations in which the psychologist feels it is to his or her advantage to explore at length the referral agent's concerns about the client or needs for additional information. The conference can be as informal as a telephone conversation in which the psychologist briefly discusses the client's problems with the referral agent in order to ascertain precisely what sort of information the agent wants about the client. As a result of this conference, the psychologist should be able to make a succinct statement of the referral problems, often in the form of a series of questions.

Here is an example of how the reason for referral can be clarified by means of a brief conference. The following was written on a referral form sent to a psychologist in a community mental health agency: "Reason for Referral: I'm referring the client for evaluation to find out information to help in therapeutic planning." This reason for referral was vague. Although the psychologist might have chosen simply to write a general description type of report in the hope that the information contained might be helpful to the referral agent, in this instance the psychologist telephoned the agent. The psychologist thanked the agent for the referral and asked whether there were any specific questions to be addressed in the evaluation report. The agent responded that her central concern was in finding out whether the child's abusive family background had affected significantly the child's emotional functioning and, if so, in what way. This brief telephone contact resulted in an important clarification of the referral problem; the referral agent had not wanted to write the sensitive information on the referral form and had not had the time to contact the psychologist directly.

Another way in which the referral problem can be clarified further for purposes of assessment is to use the Referral Problems Category System, either adult or child version. The categories within these two systems have been shown to be useful in describing both child and adult referral problems in school, hospital, and community mental health center settings (Ownby, 1986b; Ownby et al., 1984; Ownby et al., 1985; Westman, Ownby, & Smith, 1987). Use of this system allows the report writer to determine what sort of report is likely to be most effective by context and by professional to whom the report is transmitted. For example, a referral might be received from a psychiatrist who requested evaluation of a client's overall mental status. The referral problems category system (Ownby, 1986b) suggests that for a general understanding type of referral by a physician, the format of the report should be a letter (see Chapter 7 for further explanation); the model of the report should be modified hypothesis-oriented, or question-oriented; and the style should be formal professional. When the referring agent is a teacher in the public school who is asking for a general understanding of a child in his or her classroom, the category system suggests that the format of the report should be standard narrative, the model of the report should be domain-oriented, and the style should be formal professional. Although the detailed explanation of assessment findings depends on the assessment results themselves, some of the reporting variables can be determined by the nature of the referral problem and the referral agent.

Assessing the referral environment. Assessment of the environment into which the report is to be sent includes consideration of the setting in which its primary intended reader functions (for example, clinic, hospital, school, or agency); whether that setting implies that the report must be written for both primary and secondary readers (as might be true in a school setting, in which the teacher, counselor, and administrator might all read the report); and which of the several discrete functions of the report (such as communicating or providing a record of the assessment) are most important within the assessment context.

The complexity of the setting can be determined easily from knowledge of the referral agent. Settings can be rated as high, medium, or low complexity depending on the number of likely readers of various professional backgrounds by whom the report is likely to be seen. A low complexity setting might be a report sent to a physician in private practice. In this case, there is only a primary reader (the physician); because there are no secondary readers, the characteristics of varying professional backgrounds need not be considered. A high complexity setting would be a psychiatric or rehabilitation hospital that utilizes a team approach. In this case, there probably will be one primary reader and a number of secondary readers. A large number of professional disciplines probably will be represented, including medicine, nursing, occupational and physical therapy, speech pathology, and other programming specialties. The complexity of the setting will affect the way the psychologist writes the report through his or her use of language, middle-level constructs, style, and organization.

Here are complexity estimates for a number of typical settings in which psychologists might write reports:

Psychiatric Inpatient: high complexity because of the large number of secondary readers and the diversity of professional backgrounds represented. The psychologist must be concerned with both primary and secondary readers' knowledge of assessment procedures and the MLCs used in reports.

Community Mental Health Center: high complexity, again because of the large number of secondary readers and the diversity of their backgrounds.

School Setting: moderate complexity. The report is likely to be read by both the primary reader, usually the classroom teacher, and perhaps also by the counselor, administrator, or special educational specialist. Even though there are a fairly large number of potential secondary readers, their professional backgrounds are similar.

Industrial Setting: moderate complexity. In the industrial setting, the report is likely to be read by both primary readers, such as the personnel manager or assistants, as well as by secondary readers in management positions. As in the school setting, although there are a large number of potential secondary readers, their professional backgrounds are similar.

Private Practice Psychologist: *low complexity*. Even though the report might be read by several persons in a group practice, the characteristics of the primary and secondary readers will be similar, which will allow the writer to make an estimate of the readers' characteristics.

Private Practice Physician: *low complexity*. There probably will be only one primary reader and no secondary reader. The writer will be able to make an accurate estimate of the characteristics of the report's reader.

Tailoring Message Discrepancy

In this discussion, the overall purpose of the report has been defined as providing credible and persuasive statements to the report's readers. Consistent with the professional nature of psychological reports, the primary emphasis of this book has been on ways to make statements credible to readers with the explicit assumption that credible statements are most likely to be persuasive as well. This section, however, will consider ways to make statements more persuasive to their readers in additional detail. Research on the social psychology of persuasive communication (McGuire, 1985; Tedeschi & Lindskold, 1976, pp. 321-364) and the social influence theory of counseling (Strong, 1968) will be discussed.

Research in social psychology that deals with persuasive communication has focused heavily on the discrepancy of the message's content with the receiver's own belief system. In general, the research has shown that messages that are moderately discrepant from the receiver's beliefs are likely to produce the largest amount of attitude change in the receiver, although a number of factors may affect this outcome. Petty and Cacioppo (1986), for example, argue that an issue of central importance in attitude change regardless of discrepancy is the extent to which the persuasive message is processed by its receiver. Several things, such as format, attractiveness, and salience, can influence extent of message processing and, thereby, affect the persuasiveness of the communication. The implications of their model for reports are clear. The psychologist should strive to ensure the greatest degree of processing of the message because this is likely to produce the greatest attitude change (assuming that the message is correct, well reasoned, and well presented). Therefore, the report should be visually appealing, well organized with headings and subheadings, and succinct.

Beyond the issues of trying to guarantee that the report is read completely and its message extensively processed, it is clear that the message should be presented tactfully to make it more acceptable to the reader. The report's message should not be widely discrepant from the beliefs of the primary (and possibly secondary) reader in order for it to produce the largest attitude change. If, for example, the referring physician is confident that a client is not in fact experiencing anxiety, but merely complaining of anxiety in order to obtain the attention of those around him or her, it may be most effective not to make a strong statement in the report that the client is extremely anxious. Instead, you can make a statement that various test indices show that anxiety may be present and perhaps include a discussion of the alternative hypothesis that the client is merely complaining of anxiety. By considering both possibilities, the conclusions of your report will not appear as discrepant from the referral agent's own beliefs, and he or she will not be as likely to discount them.

Another example might arise in the instance of a classroom teacher who insists that a child is completely capable of learning, but for some unknown reason has chosen not to do so—often, this child is termed "lazy" by surrounding adults. Your testing, by contrast, might indicate that the child is suffering from a learning disorder of sufficient magnitude to impair the child's functioning. Here, you might tailor the message's discrepancy by reviewing the test data that show evidence of a learning disorder and by providing an extensive discussion of the effects of the probable learning disorder on the child's motivational status. In this way, the message is congruent with the beliefs of the reader with respect to observations of the child's motivational status, but discrepant with respect to etiology of motivation.

This discussion raises an important ethical problem—the extent to which the reporting of data can be tailored before the psychologist may be guilty of misrepresenting, rather than appropriately communicating, the results of the assessment. Although this a matter of professional judgment, the examples above are chosen to illustrate that tailoring the discrepancy of the message may be accomplished not so much by altering the presentation of the data themselves as by altering the context of their interpretation. This approach is consistent with another area of research on persuasive communication, that which deals with the results of including a discussion of opposing viewpoints in a persuasive message.

Investigators have shown that the impact of the message may interact with inclusion of opposing viewpoints, depending on the intelligence of the person who is receiving the message and on the likelihood that the receiver will encounter the opposing viewpoint anyway. Here, the maximum effect of including a discussion of an opposing viewpoint in a persuasive communication was shown to result when the reader was intelligent and likely to be aware of counterarguments.

As the writer of a psychological report, you can assume that most of your readers are both intelligent and likely to be aware of counterarguments—especially when they themselves have advanced them. Written in professional style, a discussion of possible opposing viewpoints probably will sound quite well-reasoned and professional to your readers. Thus, it is important for you to consider opposing viewpoints in your report writing, and this may be especially useful as a way of tailoring the discrepancy of the message to your reader's own beliefs.

Social Influence Research

A second area of relevant research is Strong's (1968) analysis of counseling as a social influence process. The close relation of counseling as an influence process to consultation as an influence process may be apparent; others have referred to consultative influence as stemming from expert and referent sources. It seems likely that similar processes are involved in persuasion in report writing. Strong suggests that the elements of interpersonal influence include expertness, attractiveness, and trustworthiness. Applied to the psychological report, this analysis provides guidance in making reports more influential. In the following discussion, expertness refers to the reader's perception of the writer's expertness and trustworthiness; attractiveness will be considered both as the reader's perception of the writer's attractiveness as well as the physical attractiveness of the report, which can be viewed as the writer's representative.

In the area of *expertness*, the writer must find ways of communicating to the report's reader that the writer is a highly trained specialist in psychological assessment whose conclusions are based on extensive training and experience. You should not set out to prove your expertness by loading the report with professional jargon — as we have seen, this approach will be counterproductive. Expertness can be communicated to the reader by writing model-based statements in professional style. Such statements will communicate to readers that you have considered test data carefully and that you are willing to communicate your interpretations in a way that shares your reasoning with the reader. This degree of openness reinforces readers' perceptions of your expertness because you are sufficiently confident of your reasoning to subject it to external scrutiny. Tailoring the discrepancy of your message appropriately to the report's intended reader is also likely to enhance the reader's view of your expertness because perceived similarity is an important aspect of positive evaluations of psychologist expertise.

Many studies have shown that perceived *attractiveness* depends on perception of similarity between the target and the perceiver. In report writing, this finding indicates that you should write the report so as to suggest that you are similar to the reader. This can be accomplished by writing in a way that utilizes the other person's constructs or, whenever possible, by emphasizing the similarity of your views of the client's functioning with those of the primary reader. If a child's teacher has observed that the child behaves quite differently toward teachers who are women as opposed to those who are men, you could include a statement such as "Assessment results are consistent with Ms. Brainstorm's observation that Peter is much more likely to disobey directives from male rather than female teachers." In this way, you have emphasized the similarity of your view of the problem with that of the agent, as well as implicitly making a positive statement about the teacher's judgment.

Sorrentino (1985) has argued for the importance of considering the visual aspects of presentations of professional writing; the importance of keeping paragraphs short was discussed in Chapter 5. Strunk and White (1979) also stress the importance of making what is presented attractive to the reader: "In general, remember that paragraphing calls for a good eye as well as a logical mind. Enormous blocks of print look formidable to a reader. [The reader] has a certain reluctance to tackle them; [he or she] can lose [his or her] way in them" (1979, p. 17). These sentiments are echoed by Hollis and Donn, who recommend that the visual qualities of the report be considered when preparing it: "Typically, a reader's overall perception and evaluation will be adversely affected by the appearance of a report. Not only must the cover have eye appeal but each page and section must entice the reader's visual sense" (1979, p. 128). These authors suggest using white space, varying type size for emphasis, and highlighting key words or ideas as ways of making the report visually appealing. Other considerations in making the report physically attractive include the use of headings to break up the possibly monotonous presentation, the use of an attractive typeface, and being sure that the quality of the typing doesn't affect the reader's perceptions.

Strong's (1968) social influence theory states that perceived counselor *trustworthiness* depends on communication of a sincere interest in the client's problems, a positive attitude toward the client's potential to be helped, and an emphatic statement about the confidentiality of the client's communications; a counselor who communicates interest in the client for personal reasons, such as curiosity, will not be perceived as trustworthy.

You can apply these suggestions to report writing by ensuring that your reports deal with the client's problems in a professional manner that clearly communicates your interest in helping the primary reader deal with them. Including a balanced description of the client's strengths and weaknesses and specific suggestions for work with the client, as discussed above, may communicate a positive attitude about the client. Communications about the confidentiality of the assessment can be made in several ways. Although it is the practice of some writers to place a statement that the report is confidential at the top of the report, it is not clear whether the benefits of this practice outweigh its distracting quality. It may not be necessary to communicate explicitly about the confidentiality of assessment data when the report is transmitted within an agency. Your concern for the confidentiality of the assessment results can be communicated to a reader who is receiving the report outside of an agency by enclosing a copy of the client's signed consent to release information form with a cover letter to the reader to remind him or her that only the psychologist can release the assessment data to another party.

Although these practices may be useful, when you are transmitting assessment information, be alert to the possibility that reminders of the confidentiality of the report may appear overwrought or condescending to other professionals who are equally aware of the confidential nature of your report. You can communicate to the reader that you are not interested in the client for inappropriate personal reasons by confining the content of the report to the assessment data, their interpretation, conclusions, and recommendations. If you confine the content of the report to the elements in the expository process model and the referral questions worksheets, it is unlikely that you will appear to be inappropriately interested in other aspects of the client's functioning.

Summary

This chapter has reviewed the assessment of the context of the report and ways to tailor the report so as to produce maximum attitude and behavior change on the part of the reader. Assessing the nature of the problem, the agent, and the environment are all important in considering how the report should be written. The referral problems category system provides a structure for considering how the nature of the problem will affect the model, format and content of the report. Determining the type of professional affiliation, the level of professional training, and the openness of agenda of the referral agent provides information that will affect the model, format, language, and content of the report. The nature of the environment, and especially the characteristics of the primary reader (the referral agent) and potential secondary readers, also will affect the report's language and content. Content suitable to a report written only for another psychologist, for example, might not be suitable for a report written to a psychologist as the primary reader, but whose secondary readers might include professionals in other disciplines.

The final section of the chapter reviewed briefly the way that social psychological research on persuasive communications and social influence can help you write the most effective report. Research suggests that the most effective report will communicate a moderately discrepant message that takes into account opposing viewpoints and that communicates the writer's expertness and trustworthiness in a format that is visually attractive to the reader.

7

ORGANIZATION AND CONTENT OF THE REPORT

This chapter presents a variety of organizations for sections of the psychological report and discusses the content that should be included in each. The various ways of organizing reports will be discussed as report *formats*, which include the business letter, the brief narrative, and the lengthy narrative. It will be seen that each format is appropriate to certain situations. The content of the report also will depend on the contextual variables, as we have already seen.

Before we turn to specific recommendations, we will review authorities' suggestions about report formats. By and large, a consensus is easy to arrive at; most authorities argue that the writer should organize the report into a number of distinct sections, such as "Reason for Referral," "Assessment Results," and so on. Authorities also agree that the report should be written as a narrative in which the writer explains important points about the assessment in sentences and paragraphs and relates test scores among themselves and to other pertinent issues, such as the client's age or life situation.

For example, Klopfer (1960) suggests that reports should include "reason for referral," "general observations," "test interpretation," and "summary" sections. Both Huber (1961) and Tallent (1976) have suggested similar formats for organizing the sections of the report. Seagull (1979) recommends a more complex organizational format that includes "reason for referral," "history," "behavior," "assessment procedures used," "results," "interpretation," "conclusion and recommendations," and "summary" sections. Hollis and Donn (1979) also recommend a somewhat more complex structure and suggest "report identification," "client or situation identification," "purpose of report," "psychological data," and "summary" as sections for reports.

It can be imagined that these citations do not exhaustively review the subject of authorities' recommendations about report organization. They are chosen to illustrate the substantial consensus that can be found—Klopfer and Huber, who were writing in the early 1960s, and Tallent, Seagull, and Hollis and Donn, all of whom were writing in the late 1970s, agree on the essential organizational format: The report's sections should include identifying information, a discussion of the reason for the assessment, a review of information sources, interpretation of the results, and a summary.

Perhaps one reason for this substantial consensus is that this report format makes sense to the reader. One reason for its making sense can be seen when we analyze the format according to the guidelines of the expository process model and in particular the dictates of the given-new contract. This contract stipulates that any element of the report must establish that something is shared in common with the reader—the shared referent—and provide new information to the reader about the shared referent—the new element. The organizational format of the report suggested here follows these stipulations closely. The given of the entire report is the client. The format suggested by these authorities establishes the given at the beginning of the report by including the client's name and identifying information. The given of the assessment is the reason for referral, which is established next in a section of its own. Additional information that needs to be shared prior to interpreting test results usually is provided at this point in the report.

After the given is established clearly, the writer can proceed to the new elements of the report—the assessment data and their interpretation. From the point of view of the given-new contract, then, the given elements at the highest level of the report organization are the "identifying information," "reason for referral," and "background information" sections of the report. The new elements in the sequence, then, are the "assessment results," "summary and conclusions," and "recommendations" sections. Thus, you can see that even at the highest level of organization within the report, the given-new contract cannot be violated; fortunately, the basic report outline recommended by virtually all authorities who have made a recommendation is consistent with the contract.

Report Formats

This section presents a review of report formats that moves from least complex (the business letter) to most complex (the lengthy narrative). Before you begin to write, you may want to make one further outline, this time either outlining the paragraphs of the letter or briefly detailing the content of the sections of the report. Although it may be possible to work directly from the EPM worksheet and the listing of referral questions and answers (suggested in Chapters 4 and 6), both the novice writer and the expert can benefit from the additional conceptual clarity induced by organizing the ideas to be presented in the report in an outline. As Woodford (1967) has suggested, there may be an intimate relation between clear writing and clear thinking. Whatever report format is chosen, and however it is organized before you begin to write, it is critical that the writer have a clear overall concept in mind before writing. (See Chapter 6 for additional discussion of this issue.)

1. **Letter.** Probably the simplest way to communicate evaluation information is to write a letter. In this situation, the psychologist communicates an account of the relevant circumstances of the evaluation, findings, and recommendations in a simple narrative format. This approach frequently is used in medical settings and is probably the most appropriate mode of conveying psychological assessment information in turn to medical personnel. Using a format similar to that used by other professionals in the same setting is one way of tailoring the report to its context, the importance of which was reviewed in the previous chapter. It may be the most effective communication because it is familiar to the reader, and its use can enhance the reader's perception of similarity between writer and reader, an element of interpersonal attractiveness related to the capacity of the report to influence the reader. While typically brief (1-2 pages), it allows for a concise description of the reason for evaluation, the way the evaluation was carried out and with what

results, and the psychologist's opinion of what the recipient's role in the treatment of the client should be.

Exactly what information is to be included in the letter is at the discretion of the writer. Because brevity is essential, the choice of information ought to be guided by its relevance to the letter's intended recipient or the need to include it in order to substantiate the recommendations for treatment. Beyond a brief introductory paragraph that identifies the client and the reason for evaluation, little else must of necessity always be included.

It may be helpful to include a statement that explains why information is being communicated if the reason is not immediately obvious, even if the referral was made by the report's intended reader. Medical personnel may be in contact with hundreds of clients in a short period of time, and it may not always be possible for them to recall quickly who the client is and why the client was assessed. Statements such as, "Suzy was referred at your request for evaluation of her behavioral difficulties," or "I am writing at the request of Ms. Smith, who believes that this evaluation information may be useful in helping you understand her son Joey" can help the recipient understand and be sympathetic toward the communication of information that he or she may not have requested.

Evaluation information itself can be presented formally or informally, depending on the needs of the situation. Even though physicians and other probable recipients of the letter are highly trained professionals in their own fields, their knowledge of psychological assessment procedures may be limited. It is often, therefore, a better practice to describe the client's performance concretely in terms of its functional significance rather than to report tests and scores; it is also better to keep the use of middle-level constructs to a minimum. An example of this sort of interpretive statement is, "Mary performed poorly on a measure that required that she repeat series of orally presented digits (WISC-R Digit Span subtest scaled score = 4, or the 2nd percentile). This suggests that Mary's difficulties in understanding oral instructions in the classroom may derive at least in part from difficulties in attention or short-term memory." The construct "short-term memory" is itself quite concrete and is illustrated thoroughly by the accompanying example.

When the assessment data have been communicated adequately to the letter's recipient, the writer should make a statement of his or her planned activity with respect to the client and, when appropriate, his or her opinion of what the other professional's actions might be. This latter statement should be made discreetly because professionals vary greatly in their willingness to accept advice from other professionals. A tactful follow-up phone call may be a better route through which to explore recommendations, particularly when the person who is receiving the letter is not well known to the writer.

The question may arise of whether a letter adequately serves the purpose of documenting assessment results. The answer to this question must be that sometimes the letter will and sometimes it will not; the purpose of the assessment and the length and detail of the letter must supply the answer to this question. In deciding whether to prepare a more detailed report, the psychologist must judge whether a letter will communicate adequately the nature, results, and recommendations that stem from the assessment.

2. **Brief narrative report**. In at least one study (Littlejohn, 1977), the narrative report was preferred to other formats by potential report recipients. The brief narrative report with recommendations, supported by face-to-face consultation when possible, is probably the format of choice for communicating most psychological assessments. This format allows for a concise yet complete description of the assessment process and for an extensive set of recommendations. Once the writer becomes accustomed to it, the brief format easily can be dictated or written in an hour or less. It will serve the purposes of communicating the assessment results, documenting the assessment for future uses, and making written recommendations to those who are working with the client. Detailed explanation of assessment efforts can be provided orally during consultation, and the report can even be written in part from notes taken for the conference.

The sections of the brief narrative report will be familiar to most psychologists and are the same for the lengthy narrative report. The difference between these two formats is, essentially, the degree of detail presented in each section. The brief report usually should be no longer than two single-spaced typewritten pages, exclusive of recommendations. The writer should aim for less than one and a half pages; then, there will be adequate space for any additions.

This economy of length can be achieved in several ways. First, the author of the report should have a clear idea of what he or she wants to say in the report—here again, the model worksheet, the referral questions worksheet, and a section-by-section outline can be useful in clarifying what is to be reported. While the psychologist may find it easy to write a great deal about test results, it may be far more difficult to report succinctly the information requested by the referring agent. Voluminous reports, while personally gratifying displays of professional diagnostic skill, are often useless to the persons who receive them. (Exceptions to this rule are noted below in the section on the lengthy narrative format). If the essence of an assessment cannot be communicated in five to seven well-written paragraphs, the author should ask him or herself whether he or she has sufficiently developed an overall concept of the evaluation results prior to writing.

A suggested outline for the sections of the narrative report is presented in Figure 6. The sections of the report include the given elements at the beginning of the report: identifying information, reason for referral, and background information. The remaining sections of the report consist of its new elements: assessment results, summary, diagnostic impression, and recommendations. Thus, the sections of the report include a brief introduction that details the reason for the assessment and provides pertinent background information. This section will deal explicitly with defining the referral problem and placing it in context, as discussed below. The rest of the report provides a narrative discussion of how the assessment was carried out (to the extent that such a discussion is necessary) and the results, conclusions, summary, and recommendations.

The following discussion is based on the premise that you have worked through the model and referral questions worksheets and are now writing the outline of the report proper. The preliminary section of the report outline guides the writer in reconsidering the context of the referral. The writer might ask him- or herself whether the context was simple or complex. For example, did the various persons who are working with the client agree on the purposes of the assessment? Are the client's physical and social environments

FIGURE 6
SECTIONS OF THE REPORT

I. Reason for Referral, including:

—-data-based statement of the reason for referral
—specific statement of questions to be answered

II. Background Information, including:

—discussion of previous evaluation results
—school or social history
—other pertinent information obtained from other sources

III. Observations, including:

—discussion of behavioral observations during testing
discussion of home, classroom, or playground behavior
linked to middle-level constructs

IV. Assessment Results, including:

—list of assessment tools with referencing abbreviations
—results in tabular or narrative form

V. Summary and Recommendations, including:

statement integrating middle-level constructs and
providing conclusions drawn from them
—statement linking conclusions to what follows, i.e., general
instructional strategy recommendations and specific activity
recommendations

factors that should be taken into account in the report? Are there important differences between the ways in which various professional personnel work with the client? Are there differences between settings, as with two different clinics or between a child's home and school?

Next, the writer should ask, "What—precisely—is the referral problem?" At this point, it may be useful to consider all aspects of the problem, both cognitive and behavioral. If the client manifests a cognitive problem, what is its impact on the client's ability to function? Persons with certain neurological disorders, for example, may exhibit memory deficits that preclude their moving about the community independently. Children with learning deficits are often unable to function in the regular educational environment. Thus, problems that appear purely cognitive in nature can have important impacts on how the client functions behaviorally.

A third consideration in the preliminary outline is to note, however briefly, what the referring party wants from the assessment and to work toward satisfying this desire to the extent appropriate. This includes a consideration of the discrepancy of the report's message from the referral agent's own beliefs as well as the congruence of your report with the agent's agenda. Is it possible or desirable to cater to the agent's beliefs and agenda, in light of the possibility that the recommendations may not be followed if they are not at least somewhat congruent with the referring agent's agenda? If there will be a discrepancy between recommendations that result from the assessment and the referring agent's wishes, what steps can be taken to help the report have maximum impact rather than simply being disregarded? Finally, the writer should determine what sort of style and format are correct in this particular context, taking into account the characteristics of the referral agent, problem, and environment.

At this point, the writer may object that these preliminaries will consume too much time and effort. You may ask, "Why add difficulties to an already arduous task?" It is likely that much of the arduousness of report writing comes from the fact that the writer has not adequately organized assessment results in an overall concept before he or she begins to write. The process of translating your ideas into written English is far simpler when the ideas are formulated clearly. As previously noted (Woodford, 1967), the relation between clear thinking and clear writing may be interactive. Taking a few moments to consider the points discussed in the model and referral questions worksheets and to write a preliminary section outline will facilitate and shorten rather than impede and lengthen the process of writing the report.

Sections of the report. After consideration of these preliminary issues, we can turn to the content of the various sections of the report. The outline suggested in Figure 6 includes notations of the types of information that should be included routinely in the appropriate sections of almost every brief narrative report. While the information recommended for inclusion in Figure 6 almost always is required, the placement of particular items may be left to the discretion of the writer. The sections presented here are, as noted, consistent with current practice and other authors' recommendations.

The report should include a section that lists information necessary for identifying the client and psychologist, and other data that may be needed for record-keeping purposes. This information typically includes: the client's name, address, and telephone number; in the case of an evaluation of a child, the child's parents' names, especially if their last name is different from the child's; the client's birthdate and chronological age; the dates assessed and by whom; and a case identification number if one is used.

The report proper begins with a section headed "Reason for Referral." This section should include a brief statement that indicates who made the referral and for what reason. The reason for referral is to be stated in as specific a manner as possible. It may be useful to quote from the referral form and from the referring person's statements during a preassessment conference. Ideally, the reason for referral will be stated in relation to observable behaviors without mediating interpretations. A statement such as, "Dr. Psyche referred Mr. Client because he states that he often feels anxious and depressed" is to be preferred to "Mr. Client was referred because of emotional difficulties." Here, the referral question is tied to something that can be observed—the client's statements that he often feels anxious and depressed. The model stresses the importance of making certain that statements about the client are based on data; this is no less true in the Reason for Referral section than it is in later interpretive sections.

This section should conclude with a brief statement of the referral questions as reformulated after reviewing the reason for referral. The distinction between referral question and reason for referral may be made clearer through the following example. Continuing with the instance cited above, the reason for referral was the complaint of the client that he often felt anxious and depressed. The referral question, as the summary statement of the Reason for Referral section of the report, then could be expressed as: "The questions to be answered in this evaluation are what might account for Mr. Client's feelings and what can be done to help him." Such a summary statement closes the preliminary section stylistically and gives the reader a clear idea of the purpose of the assessment.

Although it may be possible to consolidate the Background Information section with the Reason for Referral section, it is usually preferable to make these two separate, even though brief, sections when background information is only briefly reviewed. This practice makes the report more visually appealing by breaking what might be one long section into two shorter ones. Other information relevant to the assessment should be included in the Background Information section. This information might include a review of the results of previous psychological evaluations and other medical, physical or occupational therapy, or speech and language evaluations. Relevant information about the client's family or home situation also can be included here, although extreme tact and consideration for the client's privacy dictates that you be convinced that the inclusion of such information is necessary and will be beneficial. Important but sensitive information, such as that about family relations, can be communicated to others orally when its inclusion in the report is probably inappropriate.

Hearsay (data known only by another's report) should be labeled clearly as such by attributing it to the person from whom it was heard. This practice helps avoid the problem of converting someone's casual observation or opinion into fact by merely presenting it above a psychologist's signature. A physical description of the client is an archaic practice to be avoided except when the client's physical characteristics materially affect the evaluation. In such cases, it is best practice to include a description of the client in the section on behavior and observations, as might be the case in reporting the evaluation of a severely retarded or orthopedically handicapped child.

The next section of the report may be headed Observations or Behavior During Assessment. This section can be omitted when there are no data that substantially affect the assessment. Statements such as "Mary's classroom behavior was appropriate" or "Mr. Client was pleasant and cooperative during test administration" add little to the reader's understanding of the person assessed and unnecessarily lengthen the report. When the psychologist notes defiant outbursts or inattentiveness during a classroom observation or anxiety and depression during test administration, a statement about the behavior's possible relation to the referral problem should be made. Especially when the behavior occurs during test administration, the statement should include an estimate of the behavior's impact on the client's performance and the test's subsequent validity.

A frequent mispractice in this section, as well as in those following, is the presentation of isolated facts or behaviors that are not clearly linked to an indication of their significance. Behavioral observations may be reported, for example, without an explanation of their relevance to the client's functioning (as found by Ownby et al., 1982). As such, they are simply floating bits of data whose relation to the rest of the report is unclear. The professional's task is not merely to present observations or test scores, but also to make them understandable to the reader and to elucidate their significance for the client's functioning. Every bit of data placed in the report should have a clear link to a middle-level construct, either by contiguous placement or through the larger structure of the surrounding narrative. Classroom observation of frequent failures to stay on task, for example, might be linked to the construct "distractible" as follows: "Paul's frequently observed inability to stay on task suggests that he is distractible."

The next section of the report is headed <u>Test Results</u>. The results are presented either in tabular and narrative form or, more simply, in narrative form alone. The reporting model (hypothesis-, domain-, or test-oriented) will affect the organization of this section. While it is common to present test results in tabular form at the beginning of the section, there is little justification for this practice because it encourages the reader to ignore the interpretation of the scores that follows and tends to overemphasize the importance of numbers in isolation from the client. While it is true that many recipients of reports will both want and be able to interpret test scores, you should consider whether test scores are reported in this fashion for a reasoned purpose or simply through habit.

When test scores are not presented in tabular format, they can be used in the narrative section of the report after you have presented a list of tests and other measures used in the assessment at the beginning of the section. A useful technical detail in relation to this list is the inclusion of a test abbreviation after each element in it as a reference for later interpretations in the report narrative. If the list includes the element "Wechsler Adult Intelligence Scale-Revised (WAIS-R)," later references to the "WAIS-R" will be understood readily by the reader. This is a particularly important practice when unusual measures are included in the assessment or when the report's intended recipient may not have a working knowledge of psychological testing. Test scores, expressed in a form appropriate to the report's reader, can thus be placed directly in the body of the report or in parentheses after a statement about them. An example of this is, "John scored in the average range on the portions of the WISC-R that tap general verbal abilities (Verbal IQ = 95)." This method of referencing the middle-level construct ("general verbal abilities") to data ("Verbal IQ = 95") emphasizes the practical significance of the test score and by its structure subordinates the IQ itself to its relevance to the child's functioning.

How you divide the narrative of assessment results into sections depends on the orientation of the report. The test-oriented report may have paragraphs with headings for each test, which usually move from measures of intellectual ability to academic achievement, personality, and behavioral assessments. Domain-oriented reports can be organized around headings that name the domains judged relevant by the report writer. Such headings might include discussion of visual, auditory, linguistic, or personality domains. The hypothesis-oriented report either may eschew sections completely and rely on a statement of the hypotheses and several supporting paragraphs, or it can be organized by test or modality. In this organizational format, the statement of the hypotheses might be followed by a consideration of support for the hypotheses from each test or in each modality. In this format, the sequence of the model constituents is reversed, with constructs being followed by data.

It was noted above that certain types of information may affect differentially the reader's perceptions of the client and of his or her ability to deal with the client's problems. This consideration indicates that the test results section should include a balanced report of the client's strengths and weaknesses in order to avoid making the reader pessimistic about the client's ability to improve and the reader's ability to help the client. It also may be remembered that information about why a client has a problem may lead the reader to have a more sympathetic view of the client. This type of information might be emphasized in reports when a good rapport doesn't exist between the client and the referral agent.

The final section of the brief narrative report, headed Summary and Recommendations or Integration and Recommendations, provides a brief overview of the assessment results, a statement of general conclusions, and a set of recommendations. The first paragraph in this section should provide a logical transition from test data to recommendations by summarizing constructs introduced in the test data section. This transition may be facilitated by discussing the implications of the assessment for the client's functioning and the relevance of the findings to work with the client. For example, the first paragraph of the section might begin, "Assessment results thus show that Mr. Client is so severely depressed that he is unlikely to benefit from psychotherapy until his mood improves." Recommendations that follow this statement then could suggest that Mr. Client be hospitalized or placed on antidepressant medication as a prelude to his receiving psychotherapy.

Before you list specific recommendations, it sometimes can be helpful to include a second paragraph that states general strategies that may be useful in working with the client. For example, Mr. Client's report might include the following general strategy recommendation: "Mr. Client has a history of unhappy and hostile relations with professionals. In general, it will be helpful to work with him in a way that does not emphasize the differences between him and the professional staff, such as using nontechnical language and treating him as an equal." In reports that deal with how to teach a client educational material, it may be useful to provide suggestions about general instructional strategies for work with the client. Such a recommendation might be, "This assessment suggests that, in general, a linguistic rather than phonics-oriented approach to reading instruction may be helpful in teaching Tommy to read." This content is consistent with Keogh's (1972) suggestion that assessments that focus on learning processes rather than on psychometric deficit may be most useful to educators.

118

Including statements of this sort in this section helps the reader make the logical transition from middle-level constructs and conclusions in the "Assessment Results" to the recommendations. Another example of this sort of transition would be to move from assessment data that show that a child has a strong preference for visual strategies in reading to a suggestion that reading instruction might focus on the development of such strategies (in addition to others). Specific recommendations could, in turn, suggest activities for developing a larger sight word vocabulary with the child.

The narrative report concludes with the recommendations sections. The length of this section depends on the assessment outcome, the referral problem, and the referral agent's needs for specific guidance. In this fashion, then, the summary and recommendations section moves logically from a summary of middle-level constructs to conclusions and recommendations.

3. **Lengthy narrative report.** The lengthy narrative format is simply an expanded version of the brief narrative. In this approach, you can give free rein to your diagnostic acumen and provide the reader with an exhaustive discussion of assessment data. This format interacts with the contextual variables (referral agent, problem, and environment). The lengthy narrative report is most appropriate for the referral agent who has an interest in detailed explanations of psychological test data, such as another psychologist or a special educator. Referral problems that pose highly specific questions can be addressed best in an hypothesis-oriented report, but when the referral objective is to provide a general description of a client's functioning, the lengthy narrative may be appropriate. Finally, a complex referral environment in which many persons may read the report can dictate that a brief report be written, but when the environment is simple and the referral agent is likely to be interested, the lengthy narrative format may be used.

4. **Recommendations only**. This format allows written transmission of recommendations without accompanying confidential test data. This approach is a partial and not altogether satisfactory solution to the problems of requests for written recommendations and the necessity for safeguarding confidential assessment information. This format may be particularly useful in a highly complex referral

environment in which it is difficult to be sure precisely who will be reading the report. This format is usually not used in isolation, but in conjunction with one of the other formats. In practice, it might be possible to distribute copies of the recommendations at the same multidisciplinary staff meeting at which assessment results are presented.

Summary

This chapter has presented a discussion of several formats for report organization with suggestions for content in each section. Ways of using each of the formats to communicate assessment results in different contexts have been discussed, and recommendations about specific content for each section of the report have been made. Although this discussion has presented the report formats as though they are distinct entities, in practice you may find that you develop a report format for use in your own setting that is a hybrid of these. Alternatively, you may find that one of these formats works for most of your assessment reporting and that you do not have to change your reporting format frequently.

8

SPECIAL PROBLEMS IN THE SPECIALTIES

This chapter presents a discussion of problems in reporting that are more likely to be encountered by those who are working in the various specialty areas of psychology. The applied specialty areas considered here include the four traditionally recognized by the American Board of Professional Psychology—clinical, counseling, school, and industrial/organizational—as well as two of the new specialty areas—neuropsychology and forensic psychology. These specialties were chosen because the problems encountered by persons who work in these areas are representative of the sorts of problems likely to be encountered in any of the specialties; persons who work in other specialty areas, such as pediatric or health psychology, are likely to find material in a number of the following sections relevant to their work.

A common issue that affects reporting in the applied specialties is that psychologists frequently are called upon to communicate with persons in other professions, such as medicine or law. Psychologists must be able to function in at least two professional worlds, each with a unique approach to defining and solving problems. This can have major implications for writing reports. In no specialty is this more true than in forensic psychology, where the legal and psychological definitions of terms such as "insanity" or "competence" may be quite different.

The differences between specialty area reports and typical psychological reports, and between reports in different specialty areas, can be classified along a number of dimensions, mainly related to the purpose of the report. Reports written by clinical psychologists for other clinical psychologists, for example, may be quite different in content, organization, and style from reports written by forensic psychologists for attorneys. The organization of the following sections is to review briefly what makes each specialty different from the others, discuss the implications of these differences for report writing, and give suggestions about how to deal with problems likely to arise in the settings in which each specialty functions.

Clinical Psychology

Clinical psychology traditionally has been concerned with assessment and remediation of disordered behavior (American Psychological Association, 1981). Clinical psychologists often have worked in psychiatric settings such as those that exist in the Veterans Administration hospital system; today, they are often found working in medical contexts as well as in community and university settings.

The implications of this specialty's focus are that clinical psychologists are likely to work with persons who have long-term disabilities and to work in settings that are more medically oriented than other specialties of psychology. It is particularly likely that clinical psychologists will work in close cooperation with psychiatrists, psychiatric nurses, and psychiatric social workers because many of the clients seen by clinical psychologists also may require interventions by these specialists. Clinical psychologists who are writing reports in these settings should, therefore, be prepared to write reports that will be intelligible to highly trained medical specialists.

It should be noted in particular that while psychiatrists and other medical personnel may be familiar with personality theory, classic and modern conceptions of psychopathology, and both traditional and recent approaches to psychotherapeutic intervention, they are not always likely to be equally familiar with psychological testing. Medical personnel may not always understand basic statistical concepts crucial to the interpretation of tests. While basic medical information about a client might be mentioned only briefly in a report for a medical professional, it may be necessary for the psychologist to provide extensive discussion of quite basic concepts in psychological testing. In this situation, the pacing of the writing should be adjusted so that the more technical information is explained in greater detail and, hence, at a slower pace. You can write with fewer details about material with which medical professionals are likely to be familiar.

Another implication of clinical psychology's traditional focus on disordered behavior is that clinical psychologists often are asked to carry out detailed assessments of a client's personality functioning. This raises the issue of writing reports in language that will be appropriate to the report's intended recipient. For example, a report written in psychodynamic language that emphasizes the client's drives, defenses, and symptoms probably won't please the behaviorally oriented clinician. Thus, it is necessary for the clinical psychologist who is carrying out assessments for psychologists of different theoretical orientations to be able to communicate assessment findings in ways that the other psychologists will find both useful and meaningful. This often will require adjusting the way in which you use middle-level constructs and approach other aspects of the report, such as model and format.

The referral problem likely to be encountered most frequently in clinical psychology is assessment for psychotherapy. In addition to a consideration of problems such as anxiety, depression, or behavioral disturbances, such an assessment usually involves an extensive examination of the client's functioning in order to determine his or her ability to profit from psychotherapy. Here, it is critical for the clinical psychologist to be familiar with the referring agent's theoretical orientation. As noted above, a dynamically oriented report may be virtually useless to a behaviorally oriented clinician.

It is in this area that the middle-level constructs of clinical psychological reports may differ from those of other specialties, although it is recognized that many of the specialties of psychology may be concerned with the practice of counseling and psychotherapy and may use the constructs discussed below. Hollis and Donn (1979, pp. 41-61) discuss how the theoretical orientation of the psychologist should influence the psychological report. They present a few basic concepts about the impact of theoretical orientation on report writing that are likely to be true for most psychologists, whatever their specialty. First, Hollis and Donn suggest that every writer recognize that he or she has a personal theoretical orientation that affects how he or she writes reports. Explicit consideration of this personal orientation may help the writer avoid expressing in reports personal assumptions that may not be held in common with the report's reader. Second, they suggest that the writer should integrate his or her theoretical orientation toward personality and treatment in order to be able to write a report that is similarly integrated. A theoretically integrated report will be more likely to make sense to the reader.

Third, Hollis and Donn suggest that the report writer should modify his or her writing of the report on the basis of an understanding of the theoretical orientation of the report's intended recipient. Although this practice might be viewed as sophistry by some, who might argue that the writer is being dishonest if he or she writes a report that is inconsistent with his or her own beliefs, Hollis and Donn argue that, "the purpose of the psychological report is to communicate – not to wage philosophical wars" (p. 43). In the following sections, constructs pertinent to a number of theoretical orientations are presented in conjunction with discussion of how to utilize them appropriately.

Theoretical Orientations

What follows is not intended to be a complete listing of the theoretical orientations of psychologists. Some of the major areas of counseling and psychotherapy theory are discussed, however, in order to provide examples, and the effects of each orientation on the report are illustrated. If the theoretical orientation you are interested in is not discussed, it may be possible to generalize from these examples and apply the principles illustrated in your own writing.

Psychodynamic. In a report written for the psychodynamically oriented psychologist, the writer may be required to discuss the meaning of projective and objective personality assessment data and present an explanation of the client's central drives, conflicts, and defenses. The writer may be expected to explain the relation of scores on ability measures to the client's personality functioning as well as to provide dynamic explanations for the client's behavior during interview and testing administration.

Constructs likely to be useful in this assessment include several key concepts in dynamic psychologies, such as "drive," "conflict," and "defense." It is particularly important to keep the report's reader in mind when you are working with these concepts because even quite sophisticated readers may not agree on what a term such as "rationalization" means. As always, it will be best to provide substantial amounts of data to illustrate the meaning of the concept. The term "obsessiveness" might be rendered, for example, as, "the client's tendency to worry excessively about insubstantial details," or the term "denial" might be explained as, "the client's ability to assert that something is not true, even when faced with compelling evidence to the contrary." The following passage is from a psychodynamically oriented report about a client referred for evaluation by his therapist because of the client's classic "Type A" behavior pattern:

Results of objective and projective personality measures indicate that Mr. Strongarm is conflicted about several dynamically important issues, including dependency needs and sexual identity. He has dealt with these conflicts by developing an exaggerated masculine identity in which he demands absurdly high levels of performance from himself both at work and even in sports activities in which he engages ostensibly so that he can "relax." His primary defense against anxiety, when the character structure that he has constructed so carefully is threatened, is to verbally act out. Psychodynamic psychotherapy with Mr. Strongarm is likely to be stormy because formation of the therapeutic relation itself will threaten to expose Mr. Strongarm's strong needs to depend on and be cared for by another person.

You can see from this example that it is possible to construct a report that can provide useful information about a client's dynamics without using terms such as "oral needs" or "reaction formation." The dynamically oriented psychotherapist almost certainly will be able to understand what is said in this report, and if the report is read by other, less sophisticated readers, it is not likely to be misunderstood.

Behavioral. The report written for the behaviorally oriented therapist should communicate information about those aspects of the client's functioning that will provide the clinician with useful information in developing a behavioral intervention. Thus, the report will not focus on internal dynamics, as did the report for the dynamically oriented clinician, but on the relations of the client's maladaptive behaviors to the responses of the client's environment.

Constructs useful in communicating with the behaviorally oriented clinician include terms such as "reinforcement," "contingency," and "behavior modification treatment strategy." Communicating assessment data in these terms is likely to make the report more useful to the clinician. Here is an example of a behaviorally oriented report, completed after assessment of the same Mr. Strongarm discussed above:

> Results of this assessment show that a number of factors in his environment may reinforce Mr. Strongarm's maladaptive behaviors. His socially inappropriate aggressiveness often elicits reinforcement from his environment in the form of others acquiescing to his demands. When he aggressively demands of a subordinate that a task be done in the particular way he wishes, the subordinate is likely to do exactly what Mr. Strongarm demands. This pattern of behavior also can affect Mr. Strongarm's relation with his spouse, who may often respond to his aggressive behavior by acquiescing, even at the cost of her own wishes. Interventions with Mr. Strongarm might focus on altering the contingencies in his environment with respect to his maladaptive behavior. It might be possible to encourage others around Mr. Strongarm simply to ignore his inappropriate aggressiveness and, thereby, subject it to extinction.

Here, the report focuses not on Mr. Strongarm's internal states, but on the effects that his inappropriate behaviors have on his environment. Suggestions for interventions, therefore, also focus on the environment in finding possible strategies for altering the response contingencies that are impinging on Mr. Strongarm's behaviors.

Cognitive. The report for the cognitively oriented clinician should focus on elucidating for the report's intended reader what cognitions underlie the client's problematic behaviors. Therapists who are particularly interested in the Rational-Emotive Therapy (RET) developed by Albert Ellis (Ellis & Grieger, 1977) might desire an explanation of the client's tendency to catastrophize about minor happenings or of the "shoulds, oughts or musts" that the client says to him- or herself, which, in turn, lead to unsatisfying behavior. Those clinicians interested in the theories of Aaron Beck (1976) might desire an explanation of the ways in which the client overpersonalizes the events around him- or herself.

Cognitive constructs include a variety of terms specific to the theory of the therapies. Persons trained in RET may attach special significance to the client's "should" statements and be quite interested in how the content of such statements may affect his or her behavior.

An example of a cognitively oriented report on Mr. Strongarm follows:

Results of this assessment suggest that several faulty cognitions affect his behavior. Mr. Strongarm believes that it is critical to his happiness in life for him always to be right, always to win, and always to be the best. When these irrational beliefs are threatened by life events, he becomes anxious or depressed and reacts to these emotions with a consistent pattern of excessively competitive behavior and compulsive overwork. Related aspects of Mr. Strongarm's behavior are his near-constant smoking and occasionally excessive use of alcohol as health-damaging attempts at stress management. Treatment with Mr. Strongarm logically might focus on helping him understand and modify his irrational belief system. A related intervention would be to help him develop and implement a stress management program.

Phenomenological. Another distinct group of therapies are those based on phenomenological methods, including the person-centered therapy of Carl Rogers (Rogers, 1961), Gestalt therapy (Perls, Hefferline, & Goodman, 1951), and existential psychotherapy (Yalom, 1980). In contrast to the other therapeutic approaches discussed, the phenomenological therapies are concerned to a greater extent with the client's own perceptions of the world and the ways in which they give meaning to events in their lives. Rather than the objective approach of dynamic, behavioral, or cognitive therapies, phenomenological therapies emphasize the subjective experience of the individual. The central implication of this is that reports for the phenomenological therapist should focus primarily on clients' experience of the world and the relation of their perceptions to their behaviors. While a general description of client personality might consist of a detailed discussion of drives and defenses for the dynamic therapist, for the phenomenological therapist it should consist of a detailed explanation of how the client perceives him- or herself in the world and the ways in which these perceptions contribute to problematic behaviors.

Constructs in phenomenological therapies vary with therapeutic school. Person-centered therapists may be especially interested in the way the client experiences him or herself and in the client's willingness to risk new experiences. Gestalt therapists are most likely to want data on the client's typical distortions of interpersonal contact, termed "resistances" by Gestalt therapists. Existential therapists may be most interested in information on how the client deals with the basic issues of existence—loneliness, fear of death, and bringing meaning to his or her life. Constructs such as these are most likely to be useful in communicating with phenomenologically oriented therapists.

Here is an example of a report on Mr. Strongarm prepared for a phenomenologically oriented therapist:

> Results of this assessment indicate that Mr. Strongarm's problematic behavior may stem from basic anxiety about fears of loneliness and the lack of meaning in his life. Even though his interpersonal behavior suggests a large and varied social life, Mr. Strongarm derives little true satisfaction from these contacts. He himself says that when prevented from engaging in his very active lifestyle, as when ill, he feels empty inside and quite lonely. Although he is strongly committed to work and social activities, when he reflects on these things, he views many of them as meaningless. Thus, therapeutic work with Mr. Strongarm might focus on helping him become more aware of the ways in which his denial of anxiety has affected his behavior by impelling him into a pattern of overwork and excessive competition with and hostility toward others. Therapy then might progress toward helping Mr. Strongarm develop a lifestyle that he experiences as more authentic in terms of his true self.

Here, you can see that writing for the phenomenologically oriented therapist will require familiarity with the basic concepts of the therapeutic modality. Even such common terms as "anxiety" may have a special meaning to the phenomenological therapist—in this case, the word anxiety is related more closely to Kierkegaard's philosophy than to Freud's (Brenner, 1957). In a similar way, the term "authentic" has a meaning based in the philosophical writings of Heidegger (1949).

Although the clinical psychologist will write reports about many other topics, one that he or she is likely to encounter with some frequency is the topic of assessment for psychotherapy. This section has argued that the psychologist should be able to couch the assessment report in terms that will be meaningful to the therapist who is receiving the report. You can imagine what might happen if you were to send the phenomenologically oriented report illustrated above to a strictly behaviorally oriented clinician; this should serve as a reminder to tailor your language to the report's intended recipient.

Counseling Psychology

Counseling psychology as a specialty of professional psychology usually is concerned with the task of helping those who are already functioning adequately to function better, often in the face of normal developmental events that cause temporary maladjustment. Another task that has been addressed specifically by counseling psychologists is the assessment and reporting of vocational interests and abilities (American Psychological Association, 1981).

The implications of this focus are that although the report still addresses the client's personality and need for counseling, it will do so from the perspective that the client's difficulties are temporary and that they may have resulted from normal developmental events. An example of this type of problem might be the case of a college freshman who is experiencing difficulties in adjusting to life in a dormitory. The freshman may need guidance with dating skills, time management, and study skills—concerns that are far different from those of the clinical psychologist in the inpatient psychiatric setting.

Another implication is that the counseling psychologist may be called upon to communicate with other professionals about clients' interests in vocations and their ability to succeed in them. Few other professions have extensive knowledge of the basic concepts that underlie the vocational choice process, such as congruence of interest patterns within vocational groups or vocational choice as a developmental phenomenon. This fact may require the counseling psychologist to spend some portion of the report dealing with vocational issues or explanations of the meaning of a particular pattern of interests. It might be necessary for you to explain, for example, that an artistic pattern of interests on a vocational interest measure does not of necessity mean that the client should become a studio artist. A related problem is explaining to those naive about vocational interest assessment that interest patterns are closely related to other aspects of personality function. Clearly, the person with a strongly conventional interest pattern will behave quite differently from the person with an artistic pattern. This sort of information may be useful to the report's intended recipient.

Constructs in counseling psychology are those attached to consideration of behavior problems as normal developmental phenomena and to assessment of vocational behavior. Reports thus might include terms such as, "developmental issues," "stress-related problems," "clerical speed and accuracy," or "realistic interest pattern." As with clinical psychology, these terms have specific meanings to those trained in the specialty, and the report writer should be familiar with the terms and their underlying theory before he or she attempts to write the report of the assessment.

The following passage illustrates how behavior problems can stem from normal developmental difficulties. The client, Christina, is a 19-year-old freshman at a large state university:

> Results of this assessment show that Christina's depression is probably the result of adjustment difficulties here at Large State University. This is her first protracted experience of being away from home, and she feels overwhelmed by the tasks that confront her. In addition to adapting to the large classes and increased academic task demands, she has to make new friends and deal with dating issues. Interventions with Christina might focus first on helping her simply become aware that her problems are common to persons in her situation, so that she does not feel

depressed merely because she has these difficulties. Second, it may be useful for her counselor to help Christina develop a time management plan. This program might have the dual impact of helping her manage her time better and at the same time help her feel more in control of her life. It also may be useful for Christina to participate in one of the study skills workshops offered at the campus counseling center. Third, assertiveness training interventions might help Christina learn to deal more effectively with her roommates. Fourth, helping Christina develop skills around the issues of dating would be a substantial help in reducing her anxiety about her relations with men. Ongoing contact to support her during this time of adjustment is recommended.

Counseling psychologists work in a number of settings besides college counseling centers, including hospitals that provide rehabilitation services. In such settings, the counseling psychologist might be asked to write a report about a client's vocational interests and abilities after treatment for medical and psychological problems. The following client, Rick, is a 32-year-old veteran who has been treated successfully for posttraumatic stress disorder in addition to related substance-abuse problems:

Results of this assessment suggest that Rick might be encouraged to explore occupations in manual trades such as carpentry, metal work, welding, or other building trades. Rick's pattern of vocational interests suggests that he will prefer occupational activities that allow him to work with his hands in accomplishing something visible, such as constructing a building. Assessment of abilities and academic skills shows that Rick probably has the prerequisite skills to profit from a training program or formal apprenticeship. Rick's own statements support the test data in suggesting that these are areas that might be explored profitably. For example, when asked what he liked about previous occupational experiences, Rick immediately related how he enjoyed building with wood in the Army and in his shop classes in high school. Rick's rehabilitation counselor may find it helpful to work with him in exploring these types of work and in locating possible training programs.

Here, you can see that basic test data on occupational preference and ability have been translated into a plan that encourages the reader to help the client further develop his interests in and knowledge of specific occupations without explaining vocational choice theory at length. In addition, note that statements in the report are referenced to concrete examples.

Thus, writing a report in counseling psychology reflects the particular concerns of this specialty with assisting clients in dealing with normal developmental and vocational adjustment tasks. The report's constructs, content, and style reflect the concerns of the specialty by using terms drawn from the theories that underlie each area of endeavor and a manner of expressing ideas consistent with the issues often addressed by the specialty.

School Psychology

School psychology as a specialty traditionally has been concerned with the child in the educational environment. Although school psychologists have adopted other roles, including counselor, consultant, and organizational specialist, an important continuing focus of the work of the school psychologist during the last several years has been the individual assessment of children who are not functioning well in school.

The implication of this for reporting is that reports must focus on explanations of how a child's learning and behavior patterns influence his or her success in school. More, perhaps, than in other specialties, detailed analyses of learning patterns and of their interaction with the child's successful acquisition of academic skills are content for reports. The child's social-emotional or behavioral status also becomes important content for reports, particularly when it impinges upon the child's classroom functioning. Another implication of school psychology's tradition of providing services in schools themselves is that the psychologist has a working relation with other educational specialists, including regular and special education teachers, reading specialists, and school administrators. These are the specialists with whom the school psychologist will communicate most often: knowledge of their vocabulary and way of looking at children's problems is, therefore, essential in working with them.

Middle-level constructs in school psychology follow logically from these emphases. Their content usually deals with ability and achievement, central concerns of most school psychological assessments. Although school psychologists are by no means all behaviorally oriented, many are accustomed to working with behaviorally based interventions and programs. They will be interested in dynamic interpretations of a child's behavior less often than clinical or counseling psychologists. Behavioral data upon which an intervention might be based are more likely to be useful to the school psychologist.

The following is an illustrative passage from a school psychological report:

> Results of this assessment suggest that John's academic failures in first grade may be due to specific learning difficulties. Although his scores on measures of general ability indicate that he is probably functioning in the high average range of general intellectual ability, his scores on measures of academic achievement are much lower. It appears possible that a severe discrepancy exists between John's ability and his achievement and that he may be eligible for special educational services. These results will be brought to the attention of the school district's placement committee.

This brief passage illustrates the common concern of school psychologists for assessment data from measures of ability and achievement. The rest of the passage highlights two other important factors that affect the way the school psychological report is written. First, scores from school psychological assessment often are used in part to determine whether a child can receive special education services. Second, the passage illustrates that the psychologist often must communicate test scores to other educators on a placement team, who then will determine as a group whether the child in question is eligible to receive special education services. These two factors require that the psychologist be particularly accurate and appropriate in representing test scores in reports because they are used in making a decision that can have enormous impact on the future of the child assessed. Special education placement procedures are regulated by state and federal laws; in probably no other psychological specialty does legislative regulation have such an important effect on the psychologist's day-to-day functioning.

Industrial/Organizational Psychology

One traditional focus for industrial/organizational psychologists has been on the evaluation of current and potential employees in work settings. Although many I/O psychologists today are involved in activities other than individual psychological assessments, reporting assessments of employees is still an important function.

Here, the implications of this focus include the role of the report in communicating with business professionals and the pressure for concrete and clear answers to management decision questions. Managers may not be sympathetic to reports that include much hedging about the validity of the measures used for prediction of employee behavior (although the psychologist's duty to the employee and the organization requires that the psychologist be clear about the limits of the psychological assessment in predicting employee success or, perhaps more importantly, employee failure). Beyond answering the basic question of whether a person might be successful in a particular position, the psychologist who is evaluating employees might provide management personnel with additional useful information about the employee's strengths and weaknesses in order to help guide their decisions about the employee in the future.

Constructs in industrial psychology follow from the concerns of the specialty. Discussion of ability usually is limited to overall intellectual skill levels and to the basic academic skills necessary to perform particular types of tasks. Usually, discussion of personality function also is limited primarily to personality characteristics relevant to work with employees. In assessing management personnel, for example, one might discuss the person's concern for the welfare of subordinates, need for achievement, or capacity for good working relations with others from divergent backgrounds as aspects of personality functioning that clearly are related to the person's capacity to function as a manager.

An illustrative passage from an industrial psychological evaluation follows:

> Results of this assessment show that Jones is likely to be successful in the position of department manager. She possesses good intellectual skills and the capacity to work well with others.

Personality assessment shows that she is likely to be able to combine a strong concern for task accomplishment with an appropriate level of concern for her subordinates. Her preferred decision-making style is to gather data, to reflect for a substantial time, and then to act on the basis of her thinking; when confronted with time limits, however, she is able to make decisions without losing her poise, and there is no evidence that the quality of her work deteriorates.

This report illustrates several characteristics of the industrial psychology report. Its style is less complex than that of reports in the other specialties, in keeping with the "no nonsense" attitudes of many managers in business. Issues are addressed directly in a way that does not allow the psychologist the opportunity to clarify minor issues. The clinician accustomed to addressing the fine points of personality function or test interpretation may be uncomfortable with the directness and apparent conviction of this style, but in business (and in law, as discussed below in the section on forensic psychology) the reader of the report is primarily interested in brief direct answers to the referral question and may be annoyed and frustrated by the psychologist's well-meaning attempt to write the report of the assessment as though it were addressed to another psychologist.

Clinical Neuropsychology

Clinical neuropsychologists are employed in a number of settings, the most common of which are general medical and psychiatric facilities. Their primary task is to communicate assessment findings—indeed, many neuropsychologists do not engage in treatment activities at all. Neuropsychologists usually work with patients who have actual or suspected neurological disorders. They frequently are attached to the departments of neurology or psychiatry in medical facilities, where they may work with patients with degenerative neurological diseases, head injuries, psychiatric disorders, or with children who have learning or behavior disorders.

Because assessment is their primary task, clinical neuropsychologists are often under pressure to write many reports quickly. A second pressure for the neuropsychologist is the need to communicate the results of extensive test batteries to highly trained medical specialists. Thus, neuropsychologists are required to report quickly results of a large number of tests to persons in another profession, usually medicine. This combination of circumstances means that the neuropsychologist may be able to use very technical medical terms, but be forced to deal with concepts in psychology at a rudimentary level.

The neuropsychologist also will write reports for persons in other specialties. Depending on the clientele with whom he or she works, the neuropsychologist's reports will be read by other psychologists, speech pathologists, occupational or physical therapists, and rehabilitation counselors. In addition, reports written about children with learning or behavior difficulties may be communicated to school personnel. With such diversity of potential report recipients, the psychologist who is writing the report must be particularly cautious unless he or she knows the referring agent well.

Constructs in clinical neuropsychology grow logically from the types of symptoms that persons with neurological disorders, broadly defined, may present. Problems with learning and memory, for example, are often a concern, and neuropsychologists frequently engage in exhaustive assessment and reporting on memory function that uses terms such as "verbal and nonverbal memory," "short-term vs. long-term memory," "retrieval," and "storage." These terms have fairly specific meanings to most psychologists, but the writer of the report should be aware that the relative precision of the terms' meanings in psychology is not echoed in other professions. Here, as in virtually all other situations, the psychologist should be cautious and reference constructs to behavioral observation or test data contained in the report.

The following example illustrates several of these difficulties in reporting the neuropsychological assessment. The client is Ms. Smith, who has a neurological disorder that affects her left temporal lobe:

> Results of this assessment show that this client's complaints of memory failures are based on functional difficulties in both storage and retrieval of verbal material. Her ability to learn a list of twelve words, for example, was clearly impaired because she was only

able to repeat six of them after the list was read to her five times. This level of performance probably was not due only to difficulties in retrieving the words from memory because her recognition memory (assessed as her ability to pick out the words previously read to her from a list of words) also was impaired – only eight correct, while a normal performance probably would be a perfect twelve. Assessment of Ms. Smith's nonverbal memory for geometric figures and her incidental memory for a formboard she worked with when blindfolded indicates that her memory functioning in nonverbal areas is probably within normal limits. It may be useful for Ms. Smith to return for additional work in the cognitive rehabilitation program in our department.

You may notice that this report doesn't assume that the reader is at all sophisticated about psychological measurement. Concrete examples of the client's performance are provided each time after an evaluation of the performance is given. Particularly when you are reporting the results of learning measures, it may be useful to couch the results in terms of percentages. Many persons will not see immediately the practical implications of a client's remembering only six of twelve words, but when the report writer states that the client remembers only 50% – or one-half – of what he or she learns, the reader quickly can see that the test performance may point to a significant functional disability.

Forensic Psychology

Forensic psychologists are primarily concerned with the individual whose behavior has brought him or her into direct contact with the legal system. They may be called upon to assess whether a person with a mental disorder is competent to cooperate in his or her defense, whether a person knew the difference between right and wrong at the time a crime was committed, whether a person is ready to be released or moved to a less restrictive treatment environment, or whether a person is likely to repeat an offense after being released from confinement. Forensic psychologists often engage in professional activities other than assessment, such as psychotherapy and consultation, but reporting the results of the psychological assessment of an individual remains an important part of their work.

PSYCHOLOGICAL REPORTS

The practice of forensic psychology, perhaps more than of any other specialty, requires that the psychologist modify his or her approach to language usage in reports. This is because the forensic psychologist operates within the judicial system, in which particular words and phrases are given quite precise meanings and in which important unwanted consequences may arise if these meanings are not apprehended. The precise meaning of the phrase "reasonable certainty," for example, varies between the federal and state court systems as well as among the states. Psychological constructs, even though identical to words or phrases in law, may have different meanings. The legal definition of "insane," for example, may vary across localities and be quite different from the meaning that most psychologists would give it. Lawyers, more than any other professionals, are in the business of using language in technical ways. The rules of language usage in law are determined by a tradition that extends back at least to the time of the Magna Carta; psychologists who are working in the legal system must acquire a familiarity with the ways lawyers use language if they wish to write reports that will be useful to the persons assessed as well as in the judicial decision-making process.

Examples of other constructs in forensic psychology might include terms such as, "incompetent," "mentally ill," and "probability." These terms may have definite legal meanings that can differ from what the untrained psychologist might assume. In these cases, the psychologist simply must be sure that he or she understands how the courts in a particular jurisdiction use them. Referencing constructs to behavioral observations and test data assumes a new importance in the practice of forensic psychology. Here, the psychologist is not simply striving to convince the probably sympathetic reader. In forensic psychology, the psychologist's statements may be subjected to tests of proof that are similar to those demanded of other witnesses. Even though the psychologist's report will be submitted as expert opinion, he or she may be required to explain in detail how a conclusion was reached if called upon to testify in a courtroom proceeding. If he or she already has made reference to the basic assessment data in the report, subsequent statements in court may appear more consistent—an important factor in the psychologist's credibility as an expert witness.

The following report illustrates some of these issues. The report is written about a 23-year-old woman who attacked a stranger on the street and who now stands trial for assault.

> Results of this assessment show that Ms. Brown did not understand the nature of her acts at the time of their commission. She also states that the person she attacked was a "devil" and that she had to destroy the man or risk coming under his control. She states that if she had come under his control, he would have compelled her to engage in sexual acts that to her would have been disgraceful and personally disgusting. Ms. Brown's history of hospitalization for mental illness is consistent with this pattern of symptoms. On two prior occasions she has voiced concerns that others could control her and make her do things that were obscene. Because Ms. Brown was raised in a rather rigid moralistic home, her concerns about being forced to engage in sexual acts are even more exaggerated. It is, therefore, my opinion that Ms. Brown was mentally ill at the time of the incident and that she was not able to control her actions at that moment. It is also my opinion that she continues to be mentally ill and will be for the foreseeable future. She probably will require psychiatric care for an extended period in the future, such as might be provided at State Psychiatric Facility, where she now resides in a security unit.

This report illustrates the types of information likely to be communicated in a forensic psychology report. The client's mental status at the time a crime was committed is likely to be of interest to the court because a determination of the client's guilt or innocence often depends on establishing whether he or she knew right from wrong or was able to control his or her actions at the time of the crime. The court is also likely to be interested in the psychologist's opinion about the client's future functioning and needs for treatment. In the example above, the psychologist was able to predict with reasonable certainty that the client would continue to require hospitalization and psychiatric care. The judge might take this suggestion into account when disposing of the case by requiring the client to remain in treatment at a particular facility while the judge is given periodic progress reports about the client's improvement.

Summary

This chapter has shown that certain aspects of good report writing are consistent across specialties. The need to write clearly and to reference constructs to assessment data is present in every specialty. The discussion and examples given were not intended to be a comprehensive guide to reporting in each specialty, but to illustrate the ways in which the alert report writer can modify his or her approach when the demands of the situation require him or her to do so.

9

REVIEW
AND
FUTURE NEEDS

In this chapter the outline of reporting already presented in the introduction will be reviewed as a way of summarizing the content of this book. This review will show which factors in reporting practices have been empirically investigated and what guidance these results can give you. Figure 7 is similar to Figure 1 (see the introduction), but now illustrates which aspects of the main factors and their interactions have been tested.

Structural Variables

Several of the variables have been assessed at this level. Research shows that statements are probably more effective when they are constructed in the form dictated by the expository process model. Three studies (Ownby, 1984, 1986a, 1990b) show that statements are rated more positively when constructed with the model, regardless of the type of referral problem (cognitive vs. behavioral), the type of data used to support the statement (test vs. observational), or the setting in which the raters are employed (schools, community mental health center, state hospital, or university). These results provide substantial support for the usefulness of the model in psychological report writing.

These same studies show several interesting results about the contents of isolated statements. The study of the model with school psychologists (Ownby, 1990b) obtained a significant interaction of

FIGURE 7

COMPREHENSIVE OUTLINE OF REPORTING VARIABLES

Results of Research

I. Structural Variables

    A. *Sentences*

       1. Sequence of elements
          a. EPM vs. non-EPM
       2. Content of elements
          a. cognitive vs. behavioral MLCs
          b. test vs. observational data

    B. *Paragraphs*

       1. Sequence of elements
          a. EPM vs. non-EPM
       2. Content of elements
          a. cognitive vs. behavioral MLCs

    C. *Sections*

       1. Sequence of elements
          a. EPM vs. non-EPM
       2. Content of elements
          a. cognitive vs. behavioral MLCs

II. Organizational Variables

    A. *Models*

       1. Hypothesis-oriented
       2. Domain-oriented
       3. Test-oriented

    B. *Formats*

       1. Letter
       2. Brief narrative
       3. Lengthy narrative
       4. Recommendations only

    C. *Style*

       1. Formality
       2. Vocabulary choice
       3. Grammatic structure

III. Contextual Variables

    A. *Referral Agent*

       1. Profession
       2. Level of training
       3. Agenda
       4. Familiarity with writer

    B. *Referral Problem*

       1. Type of problem
          a. referral problems category system
       2. Clarity of problem

    C. *Referral Environment*
       1. Primary vs. secondary readers
       2. Diversity of professions of readers

model by problem type. This result shows that it may be especially important for writers to support behavioral constructs with assessment data. Another finding about the content of statements (Ownby, 1986a) was that statements based on test data were rated significantly more positively than were similar statements based on observational data. A related finding was that statements that utilized inferences about children's cognitive behavior based on observations were rated less positively than statements based on authors' judgments. Although counterintuitive, this shows that readers may find that an explicit indication that the evaluator has used his or her judgment suggests that he or she is trustworthy. It should be noted, however, that test data as evidence always were rated more positively than any other form of basic data. Conclusions from these studies suggest the following guidelines for report writing:

1. Use the **expository process model** to construct sentences.
2. Be particularly careful to support statements about clients' behavioral functioning with raw data.
3. Use test data as the most, and observational data as the least, useful types of data.

At the level of the paragraph, the model also has fared well in at least one research study (Ownby, 1990a). You may recall that paragraphs constructed on the basis of the model were virtually always preferred as more effective by a diverse group of report readers. Integration of content, structure, and problem variables has not been investigated. This leads to the following guideline:

4. Use the **expository process model** to construct paragraphs.

At the level of the sections of reports, structure and content variables have not been investigated extensively. Several studies indicated a strong consumer preference for the traditional format, however (Pryzwansky & Hanania, 1986; Wiener, 1985, 1987; Wiener & Kohler, 1986). In Chapter 4, it was noted that the traditional report format is consistent with the guidelines of the given-new contract. Given this support of research for the application of the model at the levels of sentences, paragraphs, and indirectly at the level of organization, it appears reasonable to hypothesize that the basic underlying principle of the model—the given-new contract—can be applied effectively here as well. Application of the model to sections within the report requires that paragraphs establish certain things as givens before they are used as shared referents in a succeeding paragraph and that the sections of the report follow a logical sequence as well. Hence, the following guideline:

5. Use the principle of the **given-new contract** in constructing the sections of the report and in guiding its overall organization.

The theory of reporting practices associated with the comprehensive outline illustrated in Figure 7 predicts that the structural variables should be invariant across organizational and contextual variables. Studies reviewed to this point provide limited support for this prediction. Model-based statements and paragraphs consistently are rated positively by psychologists who are working in divergent settings, including schools, community centers, and in-patient hospitals. At this time, however, no more explicit tests of this prediction have been carried out.

Organizational Variables

Little research can be cited to provide recommendations about these variables. Authorities almost always agree that some report characteristics should be tailored to the context within which the report will function, but usually these authorities have not made detailed or specific recommendations. In the comprehensive outline, the report variables that are postulated to interact with context variables are model, format, and style. Review of opinion suggests the following guidelines with respect to these variables:

6. Use the hypothesis- or question-oriented **model** when you are reporting assessments undertaken primarily for a narrowly focused issue. Use the domain-oriented model when you are reporting assessments undertaken for broader purposes.
7. Choose a **format** that reports the necessary information in the shortest, simplest, and clearest fashion possible.
8. **Model** and **format** probably interact. Use briefer formats with hypothesis-oriented reports, and longer formats with domain-oriented reports.
9. Although the professional **style** discussed in Chapter 5 should be used throughout the report, the formality and other aspects of the style should vary depending on the relation between report writer and reader. The closer the relation, the more informal the style may be, within the limits of the professional purposes of the report.

Although the theory predicts that internal-organizational variables should interact with contextual variables, little direct evidence supports this prediction. Indirect support comes from the finding that improvement in feedback mechanisms between referral agent and report writer results in improvement in reports' rated usefulness or effectiveness (Affleck & Strider, 1971; Hartlage & Merck, 1971; Ownby & Wallbrown, 1983). This finding suggests that report variables interact in important ways with context variables; the theory predicts that the context interacts mainly with organizational variables. To date, there is limited empirical support for the invariance of structural variables across contexts.

Contextual Variables

Here again, little direct research evidence can be cited to provide guidance to writers. Review of authorities suggests the following guidelines with respect to contextual variables:

10. Assess the **referral agent's** profession, level of training, openness of agenda, and your relation with the agent and tailor the report accordingly.

11. Assess the **referral problem's** degree of clarity and type. Try to make the referral problem as clear as possible. Review the problem type and tailor the report accordingly.

12. Assess the **referral environment** to determine whether there is only a primary reader or whether the environment includes diverse secondary readers. Tailor the report accordingly.

These, then, are the central guidelines that result from detailed consideration of the writing on psychological reports. Although there are only twelve of them, it is likely that your report writing will be substantially improved if they are implemented in practice. Using them will require, for example, that the structure of your sentences, paragraphs, and report sections be data-based and that the conclusions and recommendations you make in the report follow logically from your interpretation of the data. Implementing these guidelines also will ensure that you assess the report's context and tailor the report's organization to its functioning in that context.

Areas for Future Research

The comprehensive outline serves the useful purpose of pointing out what types of research remain to be done in testing the theory of psychological report writing discussed in the introduction. Some of the structural variables have been considered in research; to date, for example, it has been possible to make specific recommendations about how to structure sentences, paragraphs, and sections in the report and how best to use content. Work remains to be done in establishing more firmly that the basic structural variables are, in fact, invariant across contextual variables. It may be useful to test further the relative effects of content variables on estimates of effectiveness—it might, for example, be useful to assess whether supporting observational data with test data makes the resulting mixed content statements equally or more effective than a statement that contains only test data.

Another area that merits research consideration is the determination of the effects of structural variables on readers' actual beliefs and behaviors, rather than just on their ratings of credibility and persuasiveness. Although there probably will be a close relation between ratings, belief change, and behavior change, the failure to demonstrate such a relation is a serious weakness in studies conducted to date. A research design that could approach this issue while still using the easily implemented analogue design would be to have readers rate an imaginary client on various scales that predict the client's behavior after they have read several types of reports. Such a study also might allow investigation of the possible interactions of type of information reported with type of belief change. Here, you may recall that Schwartz's (1977) study showed that type of information reported affected reader's perceptions of a client in different ways. Although work clearly remains to be done in this area, the structural are the best researched of the three categories of reporting variables.

Research on organizational variables and their interactions with contextual variables has not proceeded as far to date. Although it may be useful to study organizational and contextual variables independently of each other, it is quite clear that at least some organizational variables interact with at least some contextual variables. Thus, research on these variables will be most fruitful if it examines interactive as well as main effects of these variables. An especially important study would focus on the interactions of report formats with profession and environmental complexity. Here, researchers might determine the preferences of various professional groups for report formats. It might be worthwhile to manipulate raters' attitudinal set in making judgments by emphasizing in instructions to reports that the report either deals with a specific question to be answered or with a broad description of the client. To judge from published opinion, it is likely that preferences for report organizations will vary with the profession of the person who is receiving the report as well as with the instructed set about the function of the report.

An area for further research that is particularly important because of its significance for practice is to determine more clearly the effects of feedback on report writers' practices, on characteristics of reports, and on client treatment. Although the importance of feedback has been demonstrated (Hartlage & Merck, 1971), relatively little information has accumulated on the process by which feedback affects reports. Research on this topic would provide empirical tests of one of the theory's basic ideas, which states that reports will become most effective when organizational variables are allowed to vary with contextual variables. Because feedback is the most precise mechanism by which this covariance can occur (another might be consideration of contextual variables by the writer without formal feedback), a study of this process may be essential to understanding how to improve reports.

Computers in Reporting

The use of computers in psychological assessment and reporting is a major focus of many recent publications (Adams & Heaton, 1985; American Psychological Association, 1986; Brown, 1984; Burke & Normand, 1987; Fowler, 1985; Hartman, 1986; Jacob & Brantley, 1987; Kramer, 1988; McCullough & Wenck, 1984; Skinner & Pakula, 1986; Thomas, 1984; Walker & Myrick, 1985). There has been a virtual explosion of articles on the subject of computers in assessment during the last several years; most have focused on a combination of three general topics: (a) providing readers with general information about the availability of computerized assessment systems; (b) expressing concerns about the statistical properties of computerized test administration and scoring systems; and (c) expressing either concerns or making specific statements on the ethical issues involved in computerized assessment and reporting.

Several of these topics are germane to report writing; certainly today most psychologists are aware at least of the potential for using computers to automate assessment activities. Potential users of computer-based reporting services should be aware that most reports generated by them have not demonstrated the validity of their interpretations. As Matarazzo points out, "To date, there is no evidence . . . that one page of the narrative descriptions is valid" (1983, p. 323; also see Matarazzo, 1986). This highlights the fact that although computers can be quite useful in scoring tests and computing various scores and indices, interpretation of test scores remains a task for the psychologist even when the computer reports a number of interpretive hypotheses.

The psychologist must interpret test data in the context of other assessment variables, such as client demographic characteristics, history, and other test results. Psychologists who use the systems should treat results from them as a professional-to-professional consultation in which the validity of particular interpretations is assessed by the psychologist who has direct contact with the client. Until computer-based interpretive systems are considerably more advanced, psychologists must use results of these programs with caution. Under no circumstances should a computer interpretation be included in a report unless it is supported clearly by assessment data or labeled clearly as speculation. To produce reports at less than this standard risks unethical behavior. As Walker and Murick point out, "Users of psychological test interpretation programs or services should be cautioned *not* to view the output of these computerized programs as psychological reports, and certainly not as the final report" (1985, p. 54). Prospective users of such reports should consult the *Guidelines for Computer-based Tests and Interpretations* published by the American Psychological Association (1986).

Another computer-related issue stems from the treatment of the expository process model in Chapter 4. This presents the possibility that the algorithm for sentences and paragraphs inherent in the model might be used by computer interpretive services to produce effective statements in computer-generated reports. Because the model guidelines are quite specific, it is conceivable that a personal computer could be used in conjunction with the model to create worksheets or even preliminary drafts of reports. The writer then could edit the machine-produced text. This use of computers is quite defensible. It amounts only to an automated writing service because interpretation of test data remains solely the responsibility of the writer. Thus, applications of the model or the comprehensive outline present intriguing, but as yet unrealized, possibilities.

Reporting Activities Other than Assessment

This book has focused explicitly on reporting assessment activities, in part because of the centrality of this function in most psychological specialties and in part to limit the discussion to a manageable area. It is recognized that most psychologists in everyday practice report other activities besides individual client assessments. Examples of such reports vary from recording the progress of therapy in notes to writing lengthy research reports. While it is possible that the elements developed in the context of assessment reporting – the given-new contract, the expository process model, the comprehensive outline of reporting practices, and the theory – might be expanded to other areas of reporting, such an expansion will require substantial additional theoretical and research development.

Conclusion

In this book, I have tried to present in distilled and useful form the results of my colleagues' and my own searches for the best ways to report the results of individual client assessments. The dearth of empirical research in general, the lack of specific evidence about important issues, and our current inability to provide more than tentative guidance about reporting may be dissatisfying to you – it is no less dissatisfying to us. As our researches continue to produce answers to the practical question, "How do I write an effective psychological report?", we move closer to the time when it will be possible to produce psychological reports based on practices grounded in empirical research rather than on opinion or tradition. We can continue to hope that this area of psychological practice will receive the attention it deserves.

APPENDIX A:
LEARNING
THE
MODEL

Writing Sentences and Paragraphs; Organizing Sections

I. Writing Sentences

As discussed in Chapter 3, writing sentences with the model requires recognizing two elements: (1) a *given*, often the client; and (2) a *new*, often a result of an assessment procedure. The given and the new can be related to each other through various grammatic constructions. Elaboration, contrast, and the absolute contruction are illustrated in Chapter 3. What follows are several more examples for practicing the skills of using the model to write sentences. These are drawn from actual reports, with information changed to protect the identity of the client. Note that the sentence you construct in this section will be used in the next section to construct paragraphs. It is probably best to write down your responses, but at least try a few of these examples if only by working them out mentally.

The following data refer to a 6-year-old boy named Morris. Data for each proposed sentence are provided, with suggested answers at the end of each section.

#1   GIVEN: Morris

NEW: WISC-R Verbal IQ = 96; Performance IQ = 77; Full Scale IQ = 85. Combine these elements into a sentence by reporting the ranges into which the scores fall (Verbal = average; Performance = borderline impaired; Full Scale = low average).

Going further with Morris' WISC-R data, the subtests were reorganized and rescored to provide factor deviation quotients. Combine these into a sentence or sentences:

#2 GIVEN: Morris

NEW: Verbal Comprehension DQ = average; Perceptual Organization = borderline impaired; Freedom from Distractibility = borderline impaired.

Another test administered to Morris was the Bender Visual-Motor Gestalt Test. Combine the following information into a sentence or sentences about these results.

#3 GIVEN: Morris

NEW: Performance was significantly below age-based expectations.

NEW: Type of errors suggested impulsivity and poor fine motor skills.

Assessment information need not always derive from tests. Sometimes, information also may arise from informal inventories or interviews. What follows are several bits of information derived from varied sources during assessment of Mary Riley, a 65-year-old referred for evaluation because of reported memory problems:

#4 GIVEN: Mary

NEW: Could not state her age

NEW: Could state the year of her birth

Here are additional data derived during assessment of Ms. Riley.

#5 GIVEN: Mary

NEW: Could state the name of the current U.S. president

NEW: Could not state the name of the previous president

NEW: Could not state the name of the current state governor

And here are still more data.

#6 GIVEN: Mary

NEW: Stated that the year was 1968 (it was 1991)

NEW: Said she was unsure of the month.

ANSWERS:

You should recognize that no one will produce exactly the same sentences from these data and that there are many correct ways of reporting test results. The following sentences are offered as suggestions.

#1: Although Morris' performance on the portion of the WISC-R that primarily taps verbal skills was in the average range, his performance on that portion which taps visuospatial skills was in the borderline impaired range. The overall result is an IQ score in the low average range. (Full Scale IQ falls in the range 79 to 91.)

#2: When the subtests of the WISC-R are reorganized according to the specific abilities assessed by groups of subtests (factor analytically derived deviation quotients), his score on the verbal portion was in the average range, while his scores on the perceptual and attentional skills sections were in the borderline impaired range. (It is recognized that the Freedom from Distractibility score may be interpreted in several ways; see Ownby & Matthews, 1985.)

#3: Morris' performance on a measure of his visual-motor skills assessed as his ability to copy geometric forms with pencil and paper (Bender) was significantly below age-based expectations. In addition, the types of errors that he made on this task, which suggested impulsivity and poor fine motor skills, were relevant to his school learning problems.

#4: Ms. Riley was unable to state her own age, although she was aware of the year in which she was born.

#5: She could report the name of the current president of the United States, but could not say who was the president before him nor could she say who is the current governor of the state.

#6: She stated that the year was 1968 (it was 1991), but was unsure of the month.

II. Writing Paragraphs

By using the given and new elements in the last section, you have constructed a group of sentences about two different clients. In this section, you can use these sentences to construct two paragraphs about these clients. You may remember that in Chapter 3, two types of paragraphs were illustrated. The type I paragraph consists of a topic sentence that includes a middle-level construct, data, and a conclusion that summarizes and explains the significance of the findings. The type II paragraph consists of a topic sentence without a middle-level construct, data, and a conclusion that does include a construct. The type I paragraph emphasizes the importance of the data for the client, while the type II paragraph emphasizes the importance of the construct, which may be a diagnosis or allow the inference of significant clinical symptoms.

Try organizing the data provided in section I above into a paragraph or paragraphs about Morris. This task also will provide you with the opportunity to try your hand at integrating data from two measures.

ANSWER:

As above, it's possible to arrive at many different correct ways of narrating the data provided. What follows is a suggestion.

Results of this assessment show that Morris presents with an unusual ability pattern consistent with difficulties in visuospatial abilities, attention skills, and planning. Although his performance on the portion of the WISC-R that primarily taps verbal skills was in the average range, his performance on the portion that taps visuospatial and manual skills was in the borderline impaired range. This pattern of abilities is consistent with difficulties in many academic subjects, such as letter and word recognition skills, as well as difficulties in completing classwork. When the subtests of the WISC-R are reorganized according to the specific abilities assessed by groups of tests (factor analytically derived deviation quotients), the pattern is still clearer. For example, Morris' score in the verbal area is in the average range, while his scores in the perceptual and attentional skills areas are in the borderline impaired range. These results are thus consistent with substantial perceptual and attentional deficits.

This psychometric impression is strengthened by inspection of Morris' performance on a measure of visual-motor skills assessed as his ability to copy geometric forms with pencil and paper (Bender). Morris' performance on this measure was far below age-based expectations; in addition, he showed many errors of a type often found among children with learning or attentional deficits.

Sentences 4, 5, and 6 above provided assessment data on Ms. Mary Riley, referred for memory problems. Try organizing those data into a paragraph. A suggested answer follows:

ANSWER:

Ms. Riley presents with significant difficulties in recent memory and orientation. For example, she was unable to state her own age, although she was aware of the year in which she had been born. She could name the current president of the United States, but could not say who the previous president was nor who is the current governor of the state. In orientation, also, Ms. Riley was impaired. She stated that the year was 1968 (it was 1991) and was unsure of the month.

III. Organizing the Sections of the Report

As discussed in Chapters 1 and 4, the use of the traditional sequence of sections in the report is supported both on theoretical and empirical grounds. Rather than provide you with large sections of several reports for you to organize, possible sentences from each section of the report are provided. Your task is to determine in which section of the report they should be placed. Answers are provided below.

Decide whether the following statements should appear in the identifying information, background information, test results, or recommendations sections:

1. Results of this assessment show that Pat probably is functioning in the average range of general intellectual ability (IQ range = 90-110).

2. Patrick Woodrow, 2341 Anyplace Lane, City

3. Previous evaluations showed that Pat probably was functioning in the low average range of general intellectual ability, prior to his receiving speech therapy services.

4. In spite of his obvious progress, it is likely that Pat will continue to benefit from special educational services.

5. Pat's scores on several measures of reading skills were at levels significantly below average (for example, Woodcock-Johnson Psycho-Educational Battery Reading cluster standard score = 65).

6. Assessment date: June 5, 1990; Psychologist: Childe Psychologist, Ph.D., Case Number 640303.

7. Based on his pattern of performance on the Verbal and Performance portions of the WISC-R, it may be helpful to refer Pat once again for speech and language evaluation.

8. Pat received language therapy services during first and second grades, after which time they were discontinued as no longer necessary.

ANSWERS:

(1) Test results; (2) Identifying information; (3) Background information; (4) Recommendations; (5) Test results; (6) Identifying information; (7) Recommendations; (8) Background information.

APPENDIX B: DIAGNOSING PROBLEMS IN YOUR REPORTS

Now that you have read the book and had an opportunity to practice using the model (assuming you have worked through the examples in Appendix A), you may want to try to improve your reports. This will require diagnosing specific problems with your own reports. This Appendix provides a number of suggestions for ways to improve the reports you already write; they are grouped in three areas: self-diagnosis, consumer feedback, and colleague feedback.

Self-diagnosis

One of the best ways to diagnose problems with your reports is to dig into your files and look at reports you wrote some time ago. When reports are no longer fresh, you can read them with a more objective eye and see difficulties you might have missed when the reports were first written. Asking yourself the following questions may be useful in the self-diagnosis process. They follow from the recommendations of the expository process model and follow each of the sections of the traditional report format.

Identifying information

Is the information supplied adequate to identify the client uniquely (e.g., name, case number, birthdate)?

Is other useful information supplied (e.g., address, telephone number, age, grade in school, school building, clinic site)?

Is information that helps identify the assessment supplied (e.g., name of the psychologist, date of evaluation)?

Is unnecessary, unimportant, or irrelevant information supplied?

Reason for referral

Is this section included and, if not, is the reason for the evaluation adequately stated elsewhere in the report?

Is the reason for the referral explained clearly in this section?

Does the explanation include sufficient information so that a rationale for the assessment is clear?

Does the section include a one-sentence summary that succinctly states the reason for the evaluation? (e.g., "The purpose of this evaluation was to determine Billy's eligibility for special education services" or "The purpose of this evaluation was to help the therapist better understand the reason for Mr. Wilbuthnot's apparently compulsive behavior.").

Background information

Is this section necessary? If not, is it included? If not necessary, can relevant information be shifted to another part of the report?

What irrelevant information can be eliminated?

What information necessary for understanding the reason for referral, results, or recommendations is omitted?

Observations

Is there a reason for this to be a separate section, or could observations be better integrated into the Assessment Results section?

Are observations sufficiently explained so that the client's behavior can be readily visualized or understood by the reader?

Are observations clearly related to the purpose of the assessment?

Are observations readily linked to later conclusions? Do you use foreshadowing appropriately when it is useful? (See glossary.)

Assessment results

Are sources of assessment information listed or otherwise clearly identified?

Are professional terms used in this section? If so, are they truly shared referents?

Are any middle-level constructs that are not shared referents anchored to behavioral description?

Are sentences clearly given-new sequences related to the client?

Are paragraphs type I, type II, or some other form?

Are constructs used effectively to link assessment data to conclusions?

Is foreshadowing used when appropriate?

Is the referral problem clearly addressed, and are any relevant questions clearly answered?

Summary

Does the summary provide a restatement of all results relevant to the reason for referral and the recommendations that follow?

Is new information added in this section? If so, is there a compelling reason why it was not provided in the results section?

Does the summary provide a logical flow to the recommendations?

Is the referral problem clearly addressed in this section also?

Diagnosis

Is this section provided when necessary?

If so, is the diagnosis provided consistent with both the data included in the report and the diagnostic criteria used (e.g., DSM-III-R)?

Recommendations

Are recommendations clearly tied to problem areas identified in the report?

Are there recommendations for each problem identified? If not, is a rationale for this omission provided in either the summary or this section?

Are recommendations explained in sufficient detail to allow the provider to carry them out?

Are any unfamiliar or professional terms used in this section? If so, are they shared referents? (e.g., "use a *linguistic approach* to reading instruction" or "use *reframing* with this client in psychotherapy").

Are specific recommendations included that address the referral problem? If not, is a rationale provided either in the summary or in this section?

Are recommendations realistic? Do they conform with the possibilities inherent in classroom teaching or psychotherapy in a college counseling center?

Overall

Is the report visually overwhelming? Are paragraphs longer than 10-12 lines?

Are sections, headings, and side headings used when effective?

Is the report neatly typed? Is is possible for the reader to quickly identify information about and answers to the specific referral problem? If useful, can the recommendations section be readily detached and circulated?

More on Self-diagnosis

Study sentences. It may be useful to study intensively a few sentences drawn randomly from the report. Can you identify the given? Are there middle-level constructs, and, if so, are they linked to descriptions?

Study paragraphs. Draw several paragraphs from your reports and identify the central topic for each. Are the elements included in each paragraph related to the central topic? If not, should they be placed elsewhere in the report, or deleted?

Consumer Diagnosis

Perhaps the simplest way to obtain feedback about your reports is to ask for readers' comments. This procedure, though, may not result in much useful information. The next best way to ask for feedback is to ask consumers to complete a brief questionnaire. All the following questionnaires are based on the basic outline provided by Ownby and Wallbrown (1983). The questions in each of the following are updated and are tailored more closely to each group of consumers. The questions may vary, but each simply involves asking readers for answers to a set of questions.

School Personnel Questionnaire

This questionnaire is intended for use in school settings, to solicit information from teachers, counselors, administrators, and others.

EVALUATION FORM FOR PSYCHOLOGICAL REPORTS

We want to find out how helpful our reports are to those who receive them. We have written the following questions so that, if you are willing, you can give us information about whether this report was helpful to you and if not, why not. This information is very important in helping us improve our services.

1. Did the report answer the referral question?

 _____Yes   _____A little   _____No

2. Did the report give you new information about the student?

 _____Yes   _____A little   _____No

3. Did the report help you develop new ideas for working with this student?

 _____Yes   _____A little   _____No

4. Were the recommendations about how to teach this child helpful?

 _____Yes   _____A little   _____No

5. Were the recommendations about how to deal with the child's behavior helpful?

 _____Yes   _____A little   _____No

6. Did the recommendations show that the person writing understood how a classroom operates?

 _____Yes   _____A little   _____No

7. Overall, how useful is this report?

 ____Very useful   ____Somewhat useful   ____Not useful

8. What information should have been included, but wasn't?

 _____

9. What terms were unclear or seemed to be jargon?

 _____

10. What suggestions would you make for improving this report?

 _____

Parent Questionnaire

This questionnaire is intended for use with parents.

EVALUATION FORM FOR PSYCHOLOGICAL REPORTS

We want to find out how helpful our reports are to the parents who receive them. We have written the following questions so that, if you are willing, you can give us information about whether this report was helpful to you and if not, why not. This information is very important in helping us improve our services.

1. Did the report answer the questions you may have had about your child?

    _____Yes   _____A little   _____No

2. Did the report give you new information?

    _____Yes   _____A little   _____No

3. Did the report help you develop new ideas for you to help your child to learn better?

    _____Yes   _____A little   _____No

4. Were the recommendations about how to teach your child helpful?

    _____Yes   _____A little   _____No

5. Were the recommendations about how to deal with your child's behavior helpful?

    _____Yes   _____A little   _____No

6. Did the recommendations show that the person writing understood the problems parents face in raising children?

    _____Yes   _____A little   _____No

7. Overall, how useful is this report?

    ____Very useful   ____Somewhat useful   ____Not useful

8. What information should have been included, but wasn't?

9. What terms were unclear or seemed to be jargon?

10. What suggestions would you make for improving this report?

Therapist/Psychiatrist Questionnaire

This questionnaire is intended for use in clinical or mental health settings, in which primary intervention is likely to be psychotherapy or medication. In clinical settings, data may be used to help therapists plan long- or short-term therapy or to help psychiatrists make decisions about symptom patterns, diagnosis, and medications.

EVALUATION FORM FOR PSYCHOLOGICAL REPORTS

We want to find out how helpful our reports are to those who receive them. We have written the following questions so that, if you are willing, you can give us information about whether this report was helpful to you and if not, why not. This information is very important in helping us improve our services.

1. Did the report answer the referral question?

   _____Yes   _____A little   _____No

2. Did the report give you new information about the client/ patient?

   _____Yes   _____A little   _____No

3. Did the report help you develop new ideas for working with this client/patient?

   _____Yes   _____A little   _____No

4. Was the discussion about what causes this client's/patient's difficulties helpful?

   _____Yes   _____A little   _____No

5. Were the recommendations about therapeutic strategy or behavior modification helpful?

   _____Yes   _____A little   _____No

6. Did the recommendations show that the person writing understoods the limitations within which you must work, such as duration and frequency of therapy sessions?

   _____Yes   _____A little   _____No

7. Overall, how useful is this report?

   ____Very useful   ____Somewhat useful   ____Not useful

8. What information should have been included, but wasn't?

9. What terms were unclear or seemed to be jargon?

10. What suggestions would you make for improving this report?

Colleague Feedback

If you work in a setting with several other psychologists, a very easy and potentially helpful source of feedback can be your colleagues. They can read your reports with an objective eye and cite examples in which your reports may be unclear or in which terms may be jargon. If you wish, you can ask one or several of your colleagues to complete the following questionnaire as well.

EVALUATION FORM FOR PSYCHOLOGICAL REPORTS

We want to find out how helpful our reports are to those who receive them. The following questions are designed to help us learn the extent to which we have been successful in communicating assessment results clearly and correctly. We have written the following questions so that, if you are willing, you can give us information about whether this report seems helpful to its intended reader, and if not, why not. We'll very much appreciate the time you take in responding. Please also feel free to add any comments you have at the bottom or on the back of this sheet.

1. Did the report answer the referral question?

   _____Yes   _____Somewhat   _____No

2. Did the report give you new information about the student/client/patient?

   _____Yes   _____Somewhat   _____No

3. Do you think that the report would help the reader to develop new ideas for working with this student/client/patient?

   _____Yes   _____Somewhat   _____No

4. Do you think that the discussion about what causes this student's/client's/patient's difficulties would be helpful to its reader?

   _____Yes   _____Somewhat   _____No

5. Would the recommendations about therapeutic strategy, behavior modification, or teaching techniques be helpful to the reader?

   _____Yes   _____Somewhat   _____No

6. Did the recommendations show that the person writing understands the limitations within which the reader must work, such as classroom procedures or the duration and frequency of therapy sessions?

_____Yes _____Somewhat _____No

7. Overall, how useful is this report?

____Very useful ____Somewhat useful ____Not useful

8. What information should have been included, but wasn't?

9. What terms were unclear or seemed to be jargon?

10. What suggestions would you make for improving this report?

APPENDIX C:
A DICTIONARY
OF BEHAVIORAL
DESCRIPTIONS

Throughout this book, the use of behavioral descriptions in place of professional terms has been advocated. This appendix provides such descriptions for some major terms, tests, subtests, and scales likely to be used in psychological reports. You should be warned that each of these operationalizations may not be appropriate for each context; a definition of intelligence that emphasizes critical thinking ability may be more relevant in an employee evaluation than in a report about a child with severe developmental disabilities. For this reason, the following descriptions should be regarded primarily as examples of how specific terms can be made more intelligible to the average adult reader without professional training rather than as a cookbook of descriptions to be plugged into your report. Also for this reason, only one major instrument or group of instruments is illustrated in the areas of intelligence and personality assessment.

Intelligence

Wechsler Scales are a series of items arranged in order of increasing difficulty to compose subscales. Each set of items within a subscale taps a relatively specific ability or set of abilities. The overlap among the client's performances on all of the subtests is assumed to reflect his or her general intellectual capacity, although individual performances on subtests can be used to better understand specific assets and liabilities. The *Verbal Scale* consists of subtests that tap the ability to understand, reason about, or explain the meanings of words. For example, the Information subtest taps the client's knowledge of a wide range of topics, while the Vocabulary subtests tap his or her ability to define the meanings of words. The *Performance Scale* includes subtests that tap visual reasoning skills or the ability to carry out tasks with one's hands. For example, the Block Design subtest requires that the client assemble geometric patterns with color plastic blocks, while the Object Assembly subtest asks the client to assemble puzzles of common objects.

Following are descriptions of each of the subtests of the Wechsler scales:

Information: This subtest may be described as tapping the client's knowledge of a wide variety of topics, which range from simple concepts about numbers to the discoveries of famous scientists.

Similarities: This subtest taps the client's ability to reason about the meanings of words, assessed as the capacity to say how two words are alike.

Vocabulary: This subtest taps the client's knowledge of what words mean by asking the client to explain them to the examiner.

Arithmetic: This subtest asks the client to solve arithmetic problems read aloud.

Comprehension: This subtest assesses the client's practical knowledge of what he or she should do in a problem situation, such as dealing with a lost child in a supermarket.

Digit Span: This subtest taps the client's ability to repeat a series of numbers.

Picture Completion: This subtest asks the client to identify missing parts in pictures.

Picture Arrangement: This subtest demands that the client arrange a set of pictures into a story that makes sense.

Object Assembly: In this subtest, the client is asked to assemble puzzles of common objects.

Block Design: This subtest requires that the client assemble geometric designs with colored plastic blocks.

Digit Symbol, Coding, Animal House: Depending on whether the WAIS-R, WISC-R, or WPPSI-R is administered, this subtest may be described as a clerical task, a substitution task, or a task that requires visual-motor skills.

Personality

The Minnesota Multiphasic Personality Inventory (MMPI, MMPI-2) is a personality assessment measure that is based on relations between the ways in which people respond to test items and the ways in which they have been observed to behave. High scores on scale 1, for example, are obtained by persons who have many concerns about bodily functions and may complain of a wide variety of vague illnesses. High scores on scale 2 are obtained by persons who are observed to be sad, "blue," or frankly depressed. Such persons also may be viewed by others as discouraged and pessimistic about the future.

Persons who obtain high scores on scale 3 often are described by their therapists as resistant to psychological interpretations of their difficulties. High scorers on scale 4 are described as manifesting hostility or anger; they often are described as having histories of difficulties with authority and histories of alcohol or drug abuse. Males who score high on scale 5 are described as having a pattern of artistic interests and to be interested in intellectual pursuits, while women with low scores on scale 5 are described as being strongly identified with traditional female roles. Persons with high scores on scale 6 are unusually sensitive to the opinions of others and at times may be frankly paranoid.

High scorers on scale 7 are described as highly anxious and inclined to think over their problems excessively. High scores on scale 8 are associated with persons who report unusual perceptual experience and who are viewed by others as unusual or as not fitting in socially. Persons with high scores on scale 9 are said to act frequently without thinking and to possess high energy levels. High scorers on scale 0 often do not enjoy socializing with others and may be described as shy or anxious around others.

The preceding descriptions, it should be emphasized, simply serve as brief descriptions of scales associated with clinical entities, such as depression and introversion. It also should be emphasized that each scale is associated with several meanings and that the preceding brief descriptions are not a substitute for thorough knowledge of the varying meanings of scales depending on clinical population and patterns of other scales. A good source for additional interpretive information is Graham's book (1982).

APPENDIX D: EXAMPLES OF PSYCHOLOGICAL REPORTS

The four complete psychological reports included in this Appendix illustrate ways to apply the principles discussed in this book in actual practice. The first example illustrates a brief report of a psychoeducational evaluation of a 5-year-old. Although in some instances a more lengthy report can be useful, this report communicates the essentials of the assessment in a way that allows persons who are working with the child to grasp the nature of his difficulties and the recommended course of action. The second example reports the assessment of a woman in an outpatient clinical setting; it shows how to address a specific request for a diagnostic opinion as well as a general request for treatment recommendations. The third example illustrates one of several approaches to reporting neuropsychological assessments, in this instance, the assessment of a child with an unusual neurological disorder. Its Recommendations section is particularly lengthy in response to specific requests from the referring psychologist. The fourth example is the report of a court-ordered assessment in a forensic setting; it shows how to address specific questions from the court and to provide treatment and placement recommendations.

All four reports actually were used in their respective settings; names, dates, and specific data have been changed to protect the clients' anonymity. The last three represent somewhat lengthy reports of the expanded narrative variety—they are longer than the page and a half recommended in Chapter 7 because they represent specific responses that require a considerable degree of detail. It is hoped that by showing how the principles of report writing are applied to real assessment problems you will be better able to apply them in your own work.

Report I—Psychoeducational

This example reports an assessment undertaken to help a public school district's placement team determine the most appropriate educational setting for a preschooler. Essential data gathered by the psychologist consistent with the school district's policies included data on the child's overall intellectual functioning (Stanford-Binet), visual-motor skills (Developmental Test of Visual-Motor Integration), and educational skills (Woodcock-Johnson). The recommendations in this report are brief and general; they reflect the focus of this report on providing a general decription of the child and specific test scores rather than on in-depth diagnostic evaluation. This report can be contrasted with the third report in this section, which includes detailed recommendations for managing behavior and academic problems with a child. Also note that this report includes a diagnosis section, a requirement of the agency for which this report was produced.

PSYCHOLOGICAL EVALUATION

Name: Michael Smith   *Case No.* 123456
Address: 3311 Pine Bluff   *Date of Birth:* 2-5-85
          City   *Chronological Age:* 5-9

Reason for Referral

Michael was referred by his teacher in the Therapeutic Preschool Class, Ms. Winona Goodstreet, who requested additional test data in order to facilitate placement decisions by the Public School District. Michael has participated in the Therapeutic Preschool Class during the past two years, and his teachers report that he has shown substantial improvement in his language skills and ability to maintain attention on educational tasks.

Michael's developmental history is significant for having been delivered by Caesarean section and having in the past been treated for a seizure disorder. At the present time, he is not on medication.

Previous evaluations in February and November suggested that Michael probably functions in the high average range of general intellectual ability (IQ range = 110-120), but that his behavior was at times a problem. Evaluation showed that Michael sometimes was described as defiant toward adults and that he has a low frustration tolerance. His diagnosis at the time of the present evaluation was attention-deficit hyperactivity syndrome.

Speech and language evaluation in February showed that Michael displayed a mild to moderate receptive language delay together with problems in auditory discrimination of speech sounds.

Assessment Results

Measures used:
Stanford-Binet Intelligence Scale, 4th Edition (SB-IV)
Developmental Test of Visual-Motor Integration (VMI)
Woodcock-Johnson Psycho-Educational Battery (WJPEB)
Draw a Person (DAP)

Results of this assessment suggest that Michael is functioning in the average range of general intellectual ability. Although his composite score on the Binet was in the range 75-83, this score may be slightly lower than Michael's actual presentation because his performances on abstract/visual reasoning and quantitative tasks were lower than the potentially more relevant score on the verbal reasoning section. Here, his score was in the range of 99-111. His score on the short-term memory section of the Binet was in the range 85-97.

Assessment of Michael's visual-motor skills as his ability to copy geometric form with pencil and paper suggests that he displays a relative deficit in this area. Michael's grasp of the pencil was awkward, and he displayed minimal ability to copy the forms of the VMI (score = 2nd percentile).

Brief assessment of the development of Michael's preacademic skills shows that he has developed the ability to recognize some letters on sight, but at this time he does not read any complete words. He also has developed basic number concepts, including rote counting and the ability to associate numbers less than five with the same number of objects.

Assessment of Michael's behavioral status through projective drawings (DAP) and observation in class and during test

171

administration suggests that he continues to display a great deal of poorly modulated activity characteristic of children with attention deficits and hyperactivity. In addition, his behavior suggests poor impulse control as well as general difficulties in cognitive organization. Although he appears both bright and perceptive, at times it was difficult to obtain his cooperation during test administration. It appears that even though Michael may want to please adults, his difficulties with attention and distractibility may make it difficult for him to do so. It is likely that he will display behavioral difficulties in large group situations, such as the typical kindergarten class.

Summary and Recommendations

Results of this assessment continue to show that Michael probably functions in at least the average range of general intellectual ability in verbal areas. When his skills in quantitative or visual reasoning areas are assessed, however, his resulting performances are at lower levels. This may be due to his general perceptual disorganization, most evident in measures of his visual-motor skills. His difficulties in impulse control and planning also contribute to these relatively lower performances.

Results of this assessment show as well that Michael should be considered a candidate for special class placement when he begins to attend public schools, as may be determined by the school district's placement committee. It is apparent that even though he has made very great progress in the Therapeutic Preschool Program, it is unlikely that he will be able to succeed in a large group situation with special attention. A suggested area for educational remediation is his visual-motor skills, which reflect a broader disorganization of visual perceptual abilities.

Diagnostic Impression

Axis I: Attention-Deficit Hyperactivity Syndrome (314.00)
Axis II: Atypical Specific Developmental Disorder
Axis III: Deferred to medical personnel

Signature

Report II—Adult Clinical

This report addresses several common problems encountered in work in clinical settings. The client was referred by her therapist in a community mental health center for treatment recommendations; the consulting psychiatrist also requested specific diagnostic information. The "Reason for Referral" section makes clear that both requests are to be addressed.

PSYCHOLOGICAL REPORT

Name: Jessie Smith   *Case No.* 11223344-0
Address: 2020 Anystreet,   *DOB:* Month, day, year
      Thistown, State   *CA:* 39-6
Telephone: 555-1212   *Date Seen:* Month, day, year
                              Psychologist: C. Linical, Ph.D.

Reason for Referral

Jessie was referred by her therapist at Community Mental Health Center, Ms. Wanamaker, as well as at the request of P. Sychiatrist, M.D. Dr. Sychiatrist requested information about Jessie: specifically, whether she might be considered to display borderline personality disorder. Ms. Wanamaker requested information about possible treatment strategies.

Background Information

Ms. Wanamaker reports, in referring to Jessie, that "her whole motivation and values seem childishly punitive; people are liked by how much they do for her; grudges for fancied or real slights are cherished forever, revenge is a major goal; insulting or 'paying back' someone is prized and gloated over as a major achievement. Is there some therapeutic strategy to help make her a happier person?"

Assessment Results

Measures used:

Wechsler Adult Intelligence Scale—Revised (WAIS-R)
Bender Visual Motor Gestalt Test (Bender)
Woodcock-Johnson Psycho-Educational Battery (WJPEB; Reading cluster)

173

Beck Depression Inventory (BDI)
Minnesota Multiphasic Personality Inventory (MMPI)
Rorschach

Results of this assessment show that Ms. Smith displays many of the defining characteristics of borderline personality disorder: She shows a pattern of unstable and intense interpersonal relationships, inappropriate and unpredictable anger, identity disturbance, and affective instability. Other defining characteristics of borderline personality disorder (impulsivity in self-damaging behaviors, physically self-damaging acts, and chronic feelings of emptiness or boredom) were not observed or reported during this assessment, but may be present. The answer, then, to Dr. Sychiatrist's question as to whether Ms. Smith might appropriately be termed borderline is a tentative "yes."

Alternative, but not mutually exclusive, aspects of her personality function to consider are her history of marriage to an abusive alcoholic and her combined, as Ms. Wanamaker reports it, "resentment and self-pity." Her ongoing attachment to an abusive man presents the possibility of dependent features in her personality functioning, and the types of difficulties she experiences in relations with others suggest passive-aggressive behaviors. All of these can coexist within the general rubric of borderline personality disorder; mixed features within a disorder are quite common, and it seems most likely that this is, in fact, what Ms. Smith presents.

Additional information that emerged from this assessment may be useful in working with Ms. Smith. Assessment of her general intellectual function indicates that she probably functions in the borderline range of general intellectual ability (WAIS-R Verbal IQ = 82; Performance IQ = 84; Full Scale IQ = 82). This level of ability implies that Ms. Smith may not be able to adapt in problematic life situations as easily as might higher-functioning persons. It also has implications for therapeutic strategy because it is unlikely that she will respond to verbal psychotherapy as readily or as positively as might a person who was functioning at higher levels in the verbal domain. This is not to say that verbal therapy with Ms. Smith is useless, but it does suggest that in working with her, vocabulary might be kept simple and that techniques that have concrete and observable aspects (such as behavioral self-recording) might be most successful with her.

Objective personality assessment (MMPI) indicates that Ms. Smith probably is experiencing levels of stress that lead her to feel a very great need for support from others. Her profile suggests an exaggerated tendency to admit to personal problems, dysphoric mood, and many subjectively unusual experiences. Such a profile often is interpreted as a "cry for help," or an indication from the client that she feels an extremely strong need for psychological assistance. In such cases, establishing a positive therapeutic relation can be a powerful factor in alleviation of some more obvious symptomatology. The establishment of such a relation with Ms. Smith, however, is likely to be complicated by her diminished capacity for mutuality in relationships as well as by her intense demands for gratification. A more thorough discussion of how to deal with the problem of relationship in psychotherapy with borderline clients is provided in the articles attached at the end of this report.

Ms. Smith's responses to the Beck Depression Inventory suggest the presence of severe depression. In the context of her overall personality structure, a history of suicidal attempts is likely, though not reported in referring her. If such a history has not been elicited, it is recommended that this issue be clarified with Ms. Smith. If antidepressant medications are used in the treatment of Ms. Smith, repeated administrations of the BDI could be helpful in charting the course of her response to medication and psychotherapy. Such repeat administrations could be accomplished easily by her staff therapist, if desired.

Ms. Smith's responses to the Rorschach suggest the possibility of impaired reality testing abilities. The content of her responses was often bizarre and morbid (for example, "a dead puppy cut up," "crabs and lobsters eating the flesh of a man"). In addition to being affectively determined distortions of her perception, these responses are consistent with severe depression and seriously impaired levels of ego function. A history of psychotic episodes is possible; here again, if this aspect of her background has not been clarified, it may be useful to do so.

Finally, as Ms. Smith is at present engaged in learning to read, I assessed her current reading skills. Although she reads at a fourth-grade level (equivalent to a percentile rank of 4 and a standard score of 74), she shows strengths in being able to reason about what she reads as a means of understanding it. It may be useful to monitor her progress in reading instruction and to support her in her efforts because this is one of the few areas in which she is making positive and successful efforts at improving her adaptive abilities.

Summary and Recommendations

Results of this assessment suggest that Ms. Smith presents many features of borderline personality disorder accompanied by dependent and passive-aggressive features. She indicates that she is extremely agitated and depressed at the present time; such extreme psychological disturbance may account for the reality testing difficulties noted. The possibility of a history of suicide attempts or overt psychotic symptomatology should be investigated if these issues have not been clarified already.

As a general therapeutic strategy, establishing a strong and positive, but judiciously intense therapeutic relation can be expected to result in a reduction of some problems. Establishing realistic expectations for the therapeutic relation, however, also should be emphasized. (See the articles attached for more specifics on this problem.)

Beyond this general strategy, a secondary goal should be to assist Ms. Smith in developing greater adaptive abilities by teaching cognitive self-control techniques, developing appropriately assertive behavior, and increasing her social skills more generally. All these activities can enhance her capacity for operating more effectively in the world, and, at the same time, they will help her develop a more positive self-concept.

A potential limiting factor in Ms. Smith's development is her borderline level of intellectual function. As already noted, this factor should not be cause for undue pessimism, but should be taken into account in choice of therapeutic language and strategy. Techniques that stress concrete and observable activities are likely to be most successful with this client.

Diagnostic Impression

Axis I: Major Depression, Recurrent (DSM-III-R 296.30)

Axis II: Borderline Personality Disorder (DSM-III-R 301.83) with dependent and passive-aggressive features.

Signature

Report III—Child Clinical/School

The next report illustrates the neuropsychological assessment of Tourette's Disorder with a child who has been manifesting attentional and behavioral difficulties in school. Notice that the psychologist who wrote the report has avoided a lengthy listing of tests administered and has preferred to write them into the body of the report. This is one way neuropsychologists, who often administer in excess of 20 separate measures for an assessment, avoid taking up a large portion of the report with a simple listing of measures used. The lengthy recommendations section of the report was included because it was to be transmitted to the school system in which the child was enrolled; in fact, it was made available to the school guidance counselor and school psychologist at a joint conference with the child's regular class teacher, tutor, and parent.

NEUROPSYCHOLOGY LABORATORY

Department of Neurology, University Hospital
Major American University, University Town, State
Name: West, Danny   *Hospital No.* 123456-7   *Date:* 5-18-91

Danny West is an 8-year, 10-month-old boy evaluated at the request of his mother, Ms. Linda West. Danny was diagnosed as having Tourette's Disorder in 1982 by pediatric specialists at the University Hospital, a diagnosis subsequently confirmed by Dr. A. K. Bernstein, an authority on Tourette's. Dr. Bernstein recommended that Danny receive a complete neuropsychological evaluation, and because of this recommendation, Ms. West contacted us. Danny's past medical history is unremarkable except for a severe illness (Roseola) at age 9 months, when Ms. West reports he ran a fever of 106 degrees for approximately 5 days. Ms. West also reports, however, that she did not notice significant changes in Danny's behavior after this illness. Danny developed noticeable facial tics and throat clearing behaviors at about age 2½ years.

Ms. West reports that Danny's tics are quite mild at present, and he has not been placed on Haldol. Significant present concerns are behavioral difficulties at school, including problems in getting along with classmates, completing work in school, and paying attention to his teacher. Our examiner reports that Danny indicated some displeasure with the length of testing (he had hoped to go to the zoo in the afternoon), but that once testing began, he was sufficiently cooperative for results of this evaluation to be considered valid. The examiner noted that Danny's attention varied with type of task and task length; in particular, it diminished with verbal tasks, which were difficult for him. She also reports that Danny responded well to praise for his efforts.

This assessment shows that Danny presents few of the neuropsychological deficits often reported to be associated with Tourette's Disorder. He probably functions in the average range of general intellectual ability and does not display the often-reported discrepancy between his performances on verbal vs. visuospatial tasks (Wechsler Intelligence Scale for Children-Revised: Verbal IQ = 92; Performance IQ = 104; Full Scale IQ = 97). His performances on several measures of visuospatial problem-solving (Raven's Matrices; Category Test) were slightly below average (consistent with others' reports of difficulties in this modality among children with Tourette's), but this finding is of equivocal significance in light of Danny's above-average performance on a measure of tactile-motor problem solving, also often below average among children with Tourette's (Tactual Performance Test).

As noted above, Danny's performance on a measure of general expressive verbal ability was average (Verbal IQ = 92), as was his performance on a measure of receptive vocabulary (Peabody Picture Vocabulary Test-Revised = 101). He also performed at grade level on a naming measure (Confrontation Naming subtest of the Clinical Evaluation of Language Function), but performed poorly on a measure of verbal learning (Verbal Paired Associates Test); he made errors that are consistent with the presence of learning difficulties. His pattern of errors on the verbal learning measure also may indicate the presence of linguistic difficulties. In light of this finding and the well-documented incidence of subtle language disturbances among children with learning and behavior difficulties, it is recommended that Danny receive a thorough language evaluation.

Assessment of Danny's academic skills suggests that current efforts in special education classes have been largely successful in helping him develop basic skills in reading and arithmetic. The academic goals outlined in his individualized educational plan for the 1991-1992 school year seem appropriate, and it appears unnecessary to add to them as a result of our evaluation.

Personality assessment through parent interview and report (Personality Inventory for Children) and interview with Danny indicate that he presents significant behavioral difficulties, which include a failure to develop age-appropriate social skills, attentional skills deficits, and, perhaps as a result of these difficulties coupled with problems in academic achievement, a negative self-concept. His present participation in a social skills group led by his elementary school counselor is completely appropriate and should continue. Other suggestions for dealing with Danny's behavior difficulties are included at the end of this report.

In summary, Danny presents few of the neuropsychological deficits often associated with Tourette's Disorder. There is some indication of minor difficulties in visuospatial problem solving, but this indication is of equivocal significance in light of his average performance on other measures that also tap this ability area. Danny probably has some difficulties in verbal learning consistent with problems in acquiring academic skills, but the special education interventions carried out with him thus far appear to have been quite successful. However, the possibility of subtle linguistic difficulties cannot be ruled out on the basis of this assessment, and a more thorough evaluation by a speech and language specialist is recommended. Such an evaluation is even more important in that a portion of Danny's social skills problems could stem from the types of linguistic difficulties known to occur among children with learning difficulties.

The following recommendations may be useful to those who are working with Danny:

1. It may be possible to improve Danny's attending by occasionally asking him, when his attention wanders, about what he's working on or how far he's progressed in the assignment. It is important in this situation to ask him to try to remember

himself, as a preliminary step to his gradually acquiring the capacity to remind himself independently to return to work.

2. Danny also may be assisted in work-related behaviors by providing him with a cue to pay attention prior to giving directions or instruction. The adult who is working with Danny might say something such as "Listen carefully," then pause, and when it is clear that Danny is attending, proceed with instruction.

3. Danny's ability to follow directions also might be strengthened by asking him to repeat directions after they are given. This process encourages him to pay close attention while he is being spoken to as well as ensuring that he knows the task to be done.

4. Danny may require frequent reminders to pay attention in class. He might be placed in the classroom near the teacher, who could arrange a nonverbal signal with him to remind him that he should pay attention. Such a nonverbal cue keeps to a minimum the negative effects of teacher attention for inappropriate behavior, but at the same time helps Danny attend appropriately to the task.

5. When demands for appropriate behavior or work performance are made on Danny, it is critical that they be enforced consistently. It is essential that Danny learn that there is no way for him to avoid behaving or performing according to the rules of the classroom. Related to this approach, it will be equally essential to provide him with praise when his behavior or performance meets the required standard.

6. When Danny's behavior is socially inappropriate, a strategy that might be helpful is to discuss his behavior and its results with him at a later date. A simple problem-solving strategy is to ask the following questions and encourage Danny to arrive at his own answers:
   a. "What happened that was a problem?"
   b. "How did you react?" or "What did you do?"
   c. "Is that how you want to react?"
   d. "How could you behave differently?"
   e. "Will you behave differently next time?"

7. Those who were working with Danny reported that when confronted with his misbehavior, he often denies that it occurred.

In this situation, the denial should be treated as any other inappropriate behavior and targeted with a negative consequence. Arguments and discussions that focus on Danny continuing to deny responsibility for his actions should be avoided, as the simple act of providing him attention for denial may make it more likely that he will deny other behavior in the future.

8. In work with Danny, it probably will be important to find and emphasize areas in which he can achieve success. Providing him with recognition in this area may help him develop a more adequate sense of self-worth based on a realistic understanding that no one is good at everything and that having difficulty with academic tasks does not mean that he is a worthless person.

9. Danny should be encouraged to stop and think for a few moments before beginning a task in order to help him develop better planning skills. It also may be possible to help Danny develop better attending skills by encouraging him to remind himself to return to work when his attention wanders.

Signature

Report IV—Forensic

The fourth report in this section illustrates how to respond to specific questions posed by legal authorities in assessing a person who had been adjudged not guilty by reason of insanity. This assessment took place about two years after she committed a murder, and the court requested an opinion about whether she should be allowed a less restrictive placement and less supervision from the court and the community mental health center. Although the court transmitted its request with a series of overlapping and at times redundant questions, each question was addressed individually in the report.

PSYCHOLOGICAL REPORT

Name: Jane Jones   *Case No.* 223344-0
Address: 234 Somestreet,   *DOB:* Month, Day, Year
            Anytown, State   *CA:* 24

Telephone: 555-1234   *Date seen:* Month, Day, Year
                                            Psychologist: H. Schrink, Ph.D.

Reason for Referral

Ms. Jones was referred for evaluation by Judge V. Just of this county's Court of Common Pleas. Judge Just noted that Ms. Jones previously had been found not guilty by reason of insanity in a shooting incident in May of two years ago. Evaluation is requested at this time to determine whether Ms. Jones can be released to a less restrictive placement.

Background Information

Ms. Benjamin, social worker for the court, provides the following information in referring Ms. Jones: "Client was found 'not guilty by reason of insanity' for the murder of a 55-year-old friend of her father 2 years ago. She was sent to the local state psychiatric facility from jail after she had been evaluated by a psychologist and a psychiatrist there. No previous psychiatric hospitalization or outpatient therapy is reported. Client stated at the time of the shooting that she shot the man in order to "save" him because she had psychic experiences of him having sex with both males and females. She also stated that he propositioned her for sex. . . . Client was born in Europe, but came to the US at age 8. . . . She currently works at a sheltered workshop (she is ordered by the court to work there). She is functioning well in her job setting, although her counselor there notes that the client almost continually smiles or laughs by herself for no apparent reason."

Assessment Results

  Sources of information

  Minnesota Multiphasic Personality Inventory (MMPI)
  Rorschach
  Thematic Apperception Test (TAT)
  Clinical Interview

Ms. Benjamin supplied a group of specific issues to be addressed in this evaluation:
  1. Ms. Jones's capacity for repeating her offense
  2. Her capacity for showing hostility

3. The nature of her relations with peers
4. Her attitude toward authority, structured or otherwise
5. Her mental status
6. Her social outlook or attitudes
7. Her adaptation to the environment
8. Her social-emotional status

Capacity for repeating her offense. Results of this assessment show that Ms. Jones continues to show a number of behaviors and thought processes characteristic of schizophrenia. (Please see section below on her mental status.) The implication of this fact is that although her current behavior is neither violent nor hostile, the basic disorder (schizophrenia) that led to her offense continues to be present. It is apparent that her current status is due to her continuing psychiatric and vocational care rather than to a substantial change in her underlying disorder. Thus, it is impossible to rule out the possibility that she might engage again in violent behaviors toward others, although it can be stated with reasonable certainty that she is unlikely to engage in such behavior if she continues to receive appropriate antipsychotic medication and remains in structured and supervised living and working situations.

Capacity for showing hostility. Careful review of Ms. Jones's record of contacts with her therapist at the community mental health center, as well as reports of her counselor at the sheltered workshop, does not show the recent occurrence of behaviors that indicate hostility toward herself or others. Ms. Jones's behavior during her interview with me, in which she was confronted on several occasions with facts she prefers not to acknowledge about her past behavior, did not lead her to become angry or hostile; in fact, she was quite well controlled. Thus, both her current reported behavior and her behavior during interview suggest that she shows little overt hostility. She appears to have controlled her emotions rather rigidly so as to exclude the possibility of overt expression of anger or hostility.

Although this indicates a capacity for self-control, her rigid management of even the suggestion of irritation with others is a poor prognostic indicator because it shows that Ms. Jones probably has learned to deal with negative feelings by denying them rather than by acting upon them adaptively. Thus, it is possible that outside of a controlled and supervised setting she might not be able to maintain this degree of control and might act upon negative feelings about others.

Relations with peers. Ms. Jones denies that she has emotionally significant relations with others. She repeatedly stated that she preferred to spend her time by herself in order to read and study. A note in her therapist's record suggests that she may have some interest in relations with men in that supervisors in the group home where she resides have noted that she has gone out in the evening to see men in the neighborhood. Both Ms. Jones's statements to me and her reported behavior suggest poor relations with peers, which would not be a source of psychological support to her in stressful situations.

Attitudes toward authority. Although Ms. Jones clearly dislikes her supervised status, her attitudes expressed during my interview with her did not appear unreasonably hostile toward authority figures. It may be speculated that she has learned to deal with the legal and mental health systems by feigning compliance; it can be said that if this speculation is true, she has learned this lesson well.

Mental status. Ms. Jones was oriented to person, place, and time during my interview with her. Her affect was somewhat flattened, but otherwise was appropriate to her situation. She did not report hallucinations or delusions nor did her behavior suggest that she was experiencing either. Her thought processes were illogical and rigid, and her principal way of dealing with any problem raised was to deny its existence. When confronted with her past behavior and its current consequences she blocked and became confused. Her mental status suggests that although her mental illness is well controlled by a combination of medical and rehabilitative interventions, it is still clearly present.

Adaptation to environment. In light of her limited psychological resources, Ms. Jones has made a good adaptation to her present environment. She has learned basic ways of dealing with others at work and in her living situation and has acquired the ability to deal with her closely supervised status without behaving inappropriately. Reports from her supervisors suggest that she performs well in a structured work setting. This pattern of adjustment indicates that continued placement in this sort of environment with very gradual loosening of restrictions at the court's discretion eventually may result in Ms. Jones's rehabilitation to a less closely supervised living situation.

Social-emotional status. Ms. Jones's overall status is thus typical of persons with controlled schizophrenia. Her long-term prognosis appears to be good with continued maintenance in a supervised setting and continued medication compliance. Ms. Jones's lack of insight into the nature of her illness, her failure to develop more adaptive ways of dealing with her emotions and with other persons, and her general reliance on denial as a way of dealing with topics she finds unpleasant all indicate that she probably will continue to require supervised living and working situations for the foreseeable future. In particular, it is reasonably likely that Ms. Jones might become noncompliant with her medication regime if she is not supervised. Should this occur, she is likely to become actively psychotic again. The consequences cannot be predicted accurately, but the possibility of violent behavior toward others cannot be ruled out. Thus, continued court supervision of Ms. Jones is indicated.

Summary and Recommendations

Results of this assessment show that Ms. Jones continues to manifest residual signs of schizophrenia even though she has made a good adjustment in supervised work and living settings. Although it is currently unlikely that she will display violent behaviors, the possibility of such behavior if she were to become noncompliant with her medications outside of her supervised setting cannot be ruled out. If she were to become actively psychotic, as might occur if she ceased to take the medications prescribed by her psychiatrist, her behavior is impossible to predict.

Therapeutic work with this client is likely to be an arduous and painstaking process. It will be very difficult to develop a positive and trusting relation with her, although this sort of relation is a necessary prerequisite to accomplishing meaningful change in psychotherapy with her. Extending unconditional positive regard for her as a person while gently and slowly confronting her on issues noted above about her emotional life and her interpersonal relations is the psychotherapeutic approach most likely to be successful with her. A useful guide to work with clients similar to Ms. Jones is a text by Karon and Vandenbos, *Psychotherapy of Schizophrenia* (1981). Another useful work is Arieti's *Interpretation of Schizophrenia* (1974). These sources are recommended for specific therapeutic techniques with guarded and denying psychotic clients.

Diagnostic Impression

Axis I: Schizophrenia, Residual Type, In Remission (295.65)
Axis II: Schizotypal Personality Disorder (301.22)

_____
Signature

GLOSSARY

Context. The *context* of the report comprises all aspects of the report's environment, including factors associated with the type of organization in which it functions and the type of person to whom it is directed.

Credible. The term *credible* is used in this book to indicate the capacity of the report *to change the beliefs or attitudes* of its readers. In studies of reports discussed in this book, participants were asked to use the term "credible" to refer to the extent to which a statement in a report led them to believe the assertion it contained.

Expository Process Model. The *expository process model* specifies that certain relations should exist between the elements of statements in reports. These include data, coordinating theoretical constructs, conclusions, and recommendations. Most broadly construed, the model provides report writers with guidance about how to make statements both *credible* and *persuasive*. See Chapter 4 for a more complete explanation of the model.

Format. Report *formats* discussed in this book describe the basic organization of report elements. Formats discussed include the letter and the brief or lengthy narrative reports, each with sections set off by headings.

Given-new contract. The given-new contract refers to the way in which speakers and listeners understand each other. In the psycho-linguistic model discussed by Clark and Clark (1977), the given-new contract requires that the speaker provide unknown information (the *new*) about something with which the speaker and listener are both familiar (the *given*). In the sentence, "Mary hit the ball" the given element is "Mary" (who is presumably known to both the speaker and the listener), while "hit the ball" is the new element. The essence of this idea is that for speakers or writers to be understood by their audience, they must be certain that they all hold some information in common.

Middle-level construct. In discussion of psychological assessments, it is often useful or desirable to coordinate basic data, such as test scores or behavioral observations, with high-level conclusions through the use of explanatory terms such as "intelligence," "anxiety," or "psychosis." These terms, lying as they do between low-level data and high-level conclusions, are called *middle-level constructs*.

Model. Reporting *models* refer to the ways in which assessment results are organized within report formats, whether test-by-test, by hypotheses about the meanings of test results for the referral questions, or by functional domains.

Persuasive. The term *persuasive* is used in this book to indicate the capacity of the report to change the behavior of its readers. In studies of reports discussed in this book, participants were asked to use the term "persuasive" to refer to the extent to which a statement in a report led them to act upon the assertion it contained.

Referral Problem Category System. A system of categories with which reasons for referral can be studied. (See Ownby, Wallbrown, D'Atri, & Armstrong, 1985, or Westman, Ownby, & Smith, 1987.)

Shared referents. This phrase denotes terms whose meanings are held in common by both speaker/writer and listener/reader. The given element in the given-new contract is typically a *shared referent*.

REFERENCES

Adams, K. M., & Heaton, R. K. (1985). Automated interpretation of neuro-psychological test data. *Journal of Consulting and Clinical Psychology, 53*, 790-802.

Affleck, D., & Strider, F. (1971). Contribution of psychological reports to patient management. *Journal of Consulting and Clinical Psychology, 37*, 177-179.

American Psychological Association. (1981). Specialty guidelines for providers of psychological services. *American Psychologist, 36*, 640-681.

American Psychological Association. (1983). *Publication manual of the American Psychological Association* (3rd ed.). Washington: Author.

American Psychological Association. (1986). *Guidelines for computer-based tests and interpretations.* Washington: Author.

Appelbaum, S. (1970). Science and persuasion in the psychological test report. *Journal of Consulting and Clinical Psychology, 35*, 349-355.

Arieti, S. (1974). *Interpretation of schizophrenia* (4th ed.). New York: Basic Books.

Bagnato, S. (1980). The efficacy of diagnostic reports as individualized guides to prescriptive goal planning. *Exceptional Children, 46*, 554-557.

Baker, H. (1965). Psychological services: From the school staff's point of view. *Journal of School Psychology, 3*, (4), 36-42.

Beck, A. T. (1976). *Cognitive therapy of the emotional disorders.* New York: International Universities Press.

Berry, K. K. (1975). Teacher impressions of psychological reports on children. *Journal of Pediatric Psychology, 3*, 11-14.

Binder, L. M. (1987). Appropriate reporting of Wechsler IQ and subtest scores in assessment for disability. *Journal of Clinical Psychology, 43*, 144-145.

Brady, H. V. (1985). A case study method of assessing consumer satisfaction with school psychology services. *School Psychology Review, 14*, 216-221.

Brandt, H., & Giebink, J. (1968). Concreteness and congruence in psychologists' reports to teachers. *Psychology in the Schools, 5,* 87-89.

Brenner, C. (1957) Appendix: The reformulation of the theory of anxiety. In J. Rickman (Ed.), *A general selection from the works of Sigmund Freud* (pp. 236-246). New York: Doubleday.

Britton, B. K., & Black, J. B. (1985). Understanding expository text: From structure to process and world knowledge. In B. K. Britton & J. B. Black (Eds.), *Understanding expository text* (pp. 1-9). Hillsdale, NJ: Lawrence Erlbaum.

Brown, D. T. (1984). Automated assessment systems in school and clinical psychology: Present status and future directions. *School Psychology Review, 13,* 455-460.

Burke, M. J., & Normand, J. (1987). Computerized psychological testing: Overview and critique. *Professional Psychology: Research and Practice, 18,* 42-51.

Clark, H. H. (1985). Language use and language users. In G. Lindzey & E. Aronson (Eds.), *Handbook of social psychology* (3rd ed.), Vol. II: *Special fields and applications* (pp. 179-231). New York: Random House.

Clark, H. H., & Clark, E. V. (1977). *Psychology and language.* New York: Harcourt Brace Jovanovich.

Clark, H. H., & Haviland, S. E. (1977). Comprehension and the given—new contract. In R. O. Freedle (Ed.), *Discourse production and comprehension* (pp. 91-124). Norwood, NJ: Ablex.

Cuadra, C., & Albaugh, W. (1956). Sources of ambiguity in psychological reports. *Journal of Clinical Psychology, 12,* 267-272.

Dana, R. H., & Fouke, H. P. (1979). Barnum statements in reports of psychological assessment. *Psychological Reports, 44,* 1215-1221.

Dickson, D. H., & Kelly, I. W. (1985). The 'Barnum effect' in personality assessment: A review of the literature. *Psychological Reports, 57,* 367-382.

Ellis, A., & Grieger, R. (1977). *Handbook of rational-emotive therapy.* New York: Springer.

Entin, E. E., & Klare, G. R. (1985). Relationships of measures of interest, prior knowledge, and readability to comprehension of expository passages. In B. A. Hutson (Ed.), *Advances in reading/language research* (Vol. 3, pp. 9-38). Greenwich, CT: JAI Press.

Forer, B. R. (1949). The fallacy of personal validation: A classroom demonstration of gullibility. *Journal of Abnormal and Social Psychology, 44,* 118-123.

Fowler, R. D. (1985). Landmarks in computer-assisted psychological assessment. *Journal of Consulting and Clinical Psychology, 53,* 748-759.

Gaddes, W. H. (1983). Applied educational neuropsychology: Theories and problems. *Journal of Learning Disabilities, 9,* 511-514.

Garfield, S., Heine, R., & Leventhal, M. (1954). An evaluation of psychological reports in a clinical setting. *Journal of Consulting and Clinical Psychology, 18,* 281-286.

References

Graham, J. R. (1982). *The MMPI: A practical guide* (2nd ed.). New York: Oxford University Press.

Gredler, G. (1987). [Review of *Psychological reports* by Raymond L. Ownby]. *Psychology in the Schools, 24,* 412-414.

Hall, C. (1983, December 6). Psychiatrists' computer use stirs debate. *Wall Street Journal,* pp. 35, 39.

Hanson, D. (1988). [Review of *Psychological reports* by Raymond L. Ownby]. *School Psychology Review, 17,* 522-524.

Harrower, M. (1965). Differential diagnosis. In B. B. Wolman (Ed.), *Handbook of clincial psychology* (pp. 381-402). New York: McGraw-Hill.

Hartlage, L., Freeman, W., Horine, L., & Walton, C. (1968). Decisional utility of psychological reports. *Journal of Clinical Psychology, 24,* 481-483.

Hartlage, L., & Merck, (1971). Increasing the relevance of psychological reports. *Journal of Clinical Psychology, 27,* 459-460.

Hartman, D. E. (1986). Artificial intelligence or artificial psychologist? Conceptual issues in clinical microcomputer use. *Professional Psychology: Research and Practice, 17,* 528-534.

Heidegger, M. (1949). *Existence and being.* Chicago: Henry Regnery.

Hollis, J. W., & Donn, P. A. (1979). *Psychological report writing: Theory and practice.* Muncie, IN: Accelerated Development.

Huber, J. T. (1961). *Report writing in psychology and psychiatry.* New York: Harper & Row.

Isett, R. & Roszkowski, M. (1979). Consumer preferences for psychological report contents in a residential school and center for the mentally retarded. *Psychology in the Schools, 16,* 402-407.

Jacob, S., & Brantley, J. C. (1987). Ethical-legal problems with computer use and suggestions for best practices: A national survey. *School Psychology Review, 16,* 69-77.

Karon, B. P., & Vanderbos, G. R. (1981). *Psychotherapy of schizophrenia.* New York: Aronson.

Keogh, B. (1972). Psychological evaluation of exceptional children: Old hangups and new directions. *Journal of School Psychology, 10,* 141-145.

Klopfer, W. G. (1960). *The psychological report: Use and communication of psychological findings.* New York: Grune & Stratton.

Kodimer, C. (1988). Neuropsychological assessment and Social Security disability: Writing meaningful reports and documentation. *Journal of Head Trauma Rehabilitation, 3,* 77-85.

Koffka, K. (1935). *Principles of gestalt psychology.* New York: Harcourt, Brace.

Kramer, J. J. (1988). Computer-based test interpretation in psychoeducational assessment: An initial appraisal. *Journal of School Psychology, 26,* 143-153.

Lacey, H., & Ross, A. (1964). Multidisciplinary views on psychological reports in child guidance clinics. *Journal of Clinical Psychology, 20,* 522-526.

Lacks, P., Horton, M., & Owen, J. (1969). A more meaningful and practical approach to psychological reports. *Journal of Clinical Psychology, 25,* 383-386.

Littlejohn, W. R. (1977). Judgments of three psychological report formats by school psychologists, teachers, principals, and school psychologist-educators. *Dissertation Abstracts International, 37,* 4992A-4993A. (Abstract).

Marrow, A. J. (1969). *The practical theorist: The life and work of Kurt Lewin.* New York: Basic Books.

Matarazzo, J. D. (1983). Computerized psychological testing. *Science, 221,* 323.

Matarazzo, J. D. (1986). Computerized clinical psychological test interpretations. *American Psychologist, 41,* 14-24.

McCullough, C. S., & Wenck, L. S. (1984). Current microcomputer applications in school psychology. *School Psychology Review, 13,* 429-439.

McGuire, W. J. (1985). Attitudes and attitude change. In G. Lindzey & E. Aronson (Eds.), *Handbook of social psychology* (3rd ed.), *Vol. II: Special fields and applications.* New York: Random House.

Mertens, D. M. (1976). Expectations of teachers-in-training: The influence of a student's sex and a behavioral vs. descriptive approach in a biased psychological report. *Journal of School Psychology, 14,* 223-229.

Moore, C., Boblitt, W., & Wildman, R. (1968). Psychiatric impressions of psychological reports. *Journal of Clinical Psychology, 24,* 373-376.

Mussman, M. (1964). Teachers' evaluations of psychological reports. *Journal of School Psychology, 3,* 35-37.

O'Dell, J. W. (1972). P. T. Barnum explores the computer. *Journal of Consulting and Clinical Psychology, 38,* 270-273.

Ownby, R. L. (1982). [Review of *Report writing in special education*]. *Psychology in the Schools, 19,* 576-578.

Ownby, R. L. (1984). The credibility and persuasiveness of psychological report statements derived from the expository process model (EPM). Unpublished data, Neuropsychology Laboratory, University of Wisconsin Hospital, Madison, WI.

Ownby, R. L. (1986a). The effects of certain variables on ratings of statements in psychological reports. Unpublished data, Kent State University.

Ownby, R. L. (1986b). *Manual for the referral problem category system, adult and child versions, experimental edition.* Unpublished manuscript available from author.

Ownby, R. L. (1990a). A study of the expository process model (EPM) with clinical and counseling psychologists. *Journal of Clinical Psychology, 40,* 366-371.

Ownby, R. L. (1990b). A study of the expository process model in school psychological reports. *Psychology in the Schools, 27,* 353-358.

Ownby, R. L., & Matthews, C. G. (1985). On the meaning of the WISC-R third factor: Relations to selected neuropsychological measures. *Journal of Consulting and Clinical Psychology, 53,* 531-534.

References

Ownby, R. L., & Wallbrown, F. (1983). Evaluating school psychological reports, Part I: A procedure for systematic feedback. *Psychology in the Schools, 20,* 41-45.

Ownby, R. L., & Wallbrown, F. (1986). Improving report writing in school psychology. In T. Kratochwill (Ed.), *Advances in school psychology* (Vol. 5, pp. 7-49). Hillsdale, NJ: Lawrence Erlbaum.

Ownby, R. L., Wallbrown, F., & Brown, D. Y. (1982). Special education teachers' perceptions of reports written by school psychologists. *Perceptual and Motor Skills, 55,* 955-961.

Ownby, R. L., Wallbrown, F., & D'Atri, A. (1984). An analysis of referral problems for a four–year period. Unpublished data, Aurora City School District, Aurora, OH.

Ownby, R. L., Wallbrown, F., D'Atri, A., & Armstrong, B. (1985). The referral problems category system: A replication. *Special Services in the Schools, 1,* 53-66.

Palmer, J. (1970). *The psychological assessment of children.* New York: John Wiley.

Perls, F., Hefferline, R., & Goodman, P. (1951). *Gestalt therapy.* New York: Dell.

Petty, R. E., & Cacioppo, J. T. (1986). *Communication and persuasion.* New York: Springer.

Pryzwansky, W. B., & Hanania, J. S. (1986). Applying problem-solving approaches to school psychological reports. *Journal of School Psychology, 24,* 133-141.

Robinson, M. L. (1974). Psychological information to teachers and its effect on student achievement. *Dissertation Abstracts International, 34,* 4999A. (Abstract).

Rogers, C. (1961). *On becoming a person.* Boston: Houghton Mifflin.

Rosenthal, R., & Jacobson, L. (1968). *Pygmalion in the classroom.* New York: Holt, Rinehart & Winston.

Rucker, C. (1967a). Report writing in school psychology: A critical investigation. *Journal of School Psychology, 5,* 101-108.

Rucker, C. (1967b). Technical language in the school psychologist's report. *Psychology in the Schools, 4,* 146-150.

Sattler, J. (1974). *Assessment of children's intelligence.* Philadelphia: Saunders.

Sattler, J. (1982). *Assessment of children's intelligence and special abilities* (2nd ed.). Boston: Allyn & Bacon.

Sattler, J. (1988). *Assessment of children* (3rd ed.). San Diego, CA: Author.

Schwartz, E. B. (1977). Teacher perceptions of children as a consequence of differing content in psychological reports. *Dissertation Abstracts International, 39,* 584A. (Abstract).

Schwartz, N. H., & Wilkinson, W. K. (1987). Perceptual influence of psychoeducational reports. *Psychology in the Schools, 24,* 127-135.

Seagull, E. A. W. (1979). Writing the report of the psychological assessment of a child. *Journal of Child Clinical Psychology, 8,* 39-42.

Shea, V. (1985). Overview of the assessment process. In C. S. Newmark (Ed.), *Major psychological assessment instruments* (pp. 1-10). Boston: Allyn & Bacon.

193

Shellenberger, S. (1982). Presentation and interpretation of psychological data in educational settings. In C. R. Reynolds & T. B. Guthrie (Eds.), *The handbook of school psychology* (pp. 51-81). New York: John Wiley.

Shively, J., & Smith, D. (1969). Understanding the psychological report. *Psychology in the Schools, 6,* 272-273.

Sinclair, E., & Alexson, J. (1986). Factor analysis and discriminant analysis of psychoeducational report contents. *Journal of School Psychology, 24,* 363-371.

Skinner, H. A., & Pakula, A. (1986). Challenge of computers in psychological assessment. *Professional Psychology: Research and Practice, 17,* 44-50.

Sloves, R. E., Docherty, E. M., & Schneider, K. C. (1979). A scientific problem-solving model of psychological assessment. *Professional Psychology, 10,* 28-35.

Smith, F. (1982). *Writing and the writer.* New York: Holt, Rinehart & Winston.

Smith, M. B. (1986). The plausible assessment report: A phrenological example. *Professional Psychology: Research and Practice, 17,* 294-295.

Sorrentino, P. (1985). Let's be technically right about technical writing. In B. Hutson (Ed.), *Advances in reading/language research* (Vol. 3, pp. 167-182). Greenwich, CT: JAI Press.

Strong, S. R. (1968). Counseling: An interpersonal influence theory. *Journal of Counseling Psychology, 15,* 215-224.

Strunk, W., Jr., & White, E. B. (1979). *The elements of style* (3rd ed.). New York: Macmillan.

Sudduth, R. S. (1976). The relative efficacy of three methods of presenting psychoeducational test data to teachers. *Dissertation Abstracts International, 36,* 7965A. (Abstract).

Sundberg, N. (1955). The acceptability of "fake" versus "bona fide" personality test interpretations. *Journal of Abnormal and Social Psychology, 50,* 145-147.

Sundberg, N. (1989). How to think and write about assessments [Review of *Psychological reports*]. *Contemporary Psychology, 34,* 66-67.

Sundberg, N., & Tyler, L. (1962). *Clinical psychology.* New York: Appleton-Century-Crofts.

Tallent, N. (1976). *Psychological report writing.* Englewood Cliffs, NJ: Prentice-Hall.

Tallent, N. (1980). *Report writing in special education.* Englewood Cliffs, NJ: Prentice-Hall.

Tallent, N., & Reiss, W. (1959a). Multidisciplinary views on the preparation of written clinical psychological reports: I. Spontaneous suggestions for content. *Journal of Clinical Psychology, 15,* 218-221.

Tallent, N., & Reiss, W. (1959b). Multidisciplinary views on the preparation of written clinical psychological reports: II. Acceptability of certain common content variables and styles of expression. *Journal of Clinical Psychology, 15,* 273-274.

Tallent, N., & Reiss, W. (1959c). Multidisciplinary views on the preparation of written clinical psychological reports: III. The trouble with psychological reports. *Journal of Clinical Psychology, 15,* 444-446.

References

Taylor, J. L., & Teicher, A. (1946). A clinical approach to reporting psychological test data. *Journal of Clinical Psychology, 2*, 323-332.

Tedeschi, J. T., & Lindskold, S. (1976). *Social psychology.* New York: John Wiley.

Thomas, A. (1984). Issues and concerns for microcomputer uses in school psychology. *School Psychology Review, 13*, 469-472.

Tierney, R. J., & LaZansky, S. (1980). The rights and responsibilities of readers and writers: A contractual agreement. *Language Arts, 57*, 606-613.

Walker, N. W., & Myrick, C. C. (1985). Ethical considerations in the use of computers in psychological testing and assessment. *Journal of School Psychology, 23*, 51-57.

Waugh, R. (1970). On reporting the findings of a diagnostic center. *Journal of Learning Disabilities, 3*, 629-634.

Weddig, R. R. (1984). Parental interpretation of psychoeducational reports. *Psychology in the Schools, 21*, 477-481.

Westman, J., Ownby, R. L., & Smith, S. (1987). An analysis of 180 children referred to a university hospital learning disabilities service. *Child Psychiatry and Human Development, 17*, 275-282.

Wiener, J. (1985). Teachers' comprehension of psychological reports. *Psychology in the Schools, 22*, 60-64.

Wiener, J. (1987). Factors affecting educators' comprehension of psychological reports. *Psychology in the Schools, 24*, 116-126.

Wiener, J., & Kohler, S. (1986). Parents' comprehension of psychological reports. *Psychology in the Schools, 23*, 265-269.

Witt, J. C., Moe, G., Gutkin, T. B., & Andrews, L. (1984). The effect of saying the same thing in different ways: The problem of language and jargon in school-based consultation. *Journal of School Psychology, 22*, 361-367.

Woodford, F. P. (1967). Sounder thinking through clearer writing. *Science, 156*, 743-745.

Yalom, I. D. (1980). *Existential psychotherapy.* New York: Basic Books.

INDEX

PSYCHOLOGICAL REPORTS